BOOK BOSS

Musings from a Self-Publisher on How to Write, Publish and Market Your Own Book

SAM PEARCE

Copyright © Sam Pearce 2023. All rights reserved.

This book or any portion thereof may not be reproduced or used in any manner whatsoever without the express written permission of the publisher except for the use of brief quotations in a book review.

Strenuous attempts have been made to credit all copyrighted materials used in this book. All such materials and trademarks, which are referenced in this book, are the full property of their respective copyright owners. Every effort has been made to obtain copyright permission for material quoted in this book. Any omissions will be rectified in future editions.

Cover image by: Sam Pearce
Book design by: SWATT Books Ltd

Printed in the United Kingdom
First Printing, 2023

ISBN: 978-1-9160776-6-9 (Paperback)
ISBN: 978-1-9160776-7-6 (eBook)

SWATT Books Ltd
Amesbury, Salisbury SP4 7AR

SWATT-Books.co.uk

Contents

Introduction — 7

Part 1: ...on Writing — 9

5 Common Roadblocks to Becoming an Author &
How to Overcome Them — 10
The Most Important Question to Ask as an Author — 16
Finding the Courage to Tell Your Personal Story — 19
5 Questions to Ask Yourself When Building
Your Ideal Reader Avatar — 24
How a Publishing Plan Helped Me Publish a Great Book — 29
How I Wrote My Book in Just 30mins a Day — 34
How to Write an Amazing Book Publishing Plan — 40

Part 2: ...on Book Design — 47

Why Cheap Book Design Can Be Bad — 48
Book Design Secrets from a Professional Book Designer — 52
Book Formatting Faux-Pas: 13 Common Typesetting Mistakes — 55
5 Common Book Design Mistakes & How to Avoid Them — 66
The Science of How We Read and How to
Use it to Build a Better Book — 74
Why Font Choice is So Important in Book Design — 82
10 Best Fonts to Make Your Book Look Like a Bestseller — 94
5 Word Manuscript Tips to Save Time when
Typesetting Your Book — 108
4 Great Book Design Resources if you're on a Budget — 114
5 Keys to a Killer Book Cover — 120
How to Write a Kick-Ass Book Cover Design Brief — 125

Part 3: ...on Publishing 131

50 Shades of Self-Publishing	132
5 Pitfalls of Traditional Publishing: What Every Author Should Know	136
5 Self-Publishing Mistakes & How to Avoid Them	139
Common Self-Publishing Mistakes	145
How Long Does it Actually Take to Self-Publish a Competitive Book?	152
How Much Should It Cost to Self-Publish Effectively?	157
What Is Self-Publishing Management	165
5 Self-Publishing Resources You Need to Publish a Quality Book	168
Book Metadata: The Ultimate What, Why & How Guide	173
Cracking the Code: How to Choose the Best Category for Your Book on Amazon	185
3 Factors to Consider When Setting an Attractive Cover Price	188
ISBN Numbers: Everything You Need to Know	193
Choosing the Best Self-Publishing Platform for You: Amazon KDP vs IngramSpark	198
Book Distribution: How to 'Go Wide'	201
Copyright in Self-Publishing: What You Need to Know	204
What You Need to Know About Legal Deposits	213
3 Simple Rules for Awesome Book Marketing on Social Media	217
What Happens to Your Royalties After You Die?	221

Part 4: ...on Authorpreneurship 225

Why More Authors are Choosing to Self-Publish	226
Publishing for Entrepreneurs	232
Self-Publish or Publisher: Which is Best for You	238
Self-Publishing Triumph: 5 Books That Prove You Can Make It on Your Own	246
5 Powerful Ways to Measure Self-Publishing ROI	249
5 Ways a Book Can Boost Your Credibility	254
Authenticity: how to be genuine when you speak as an author	258
Can You Make Money from Self-Publishing?	262
Self-Publishing: When to Scrimp and When to Spend	267
How I Used my Book to Get on the Radio	275

Top 5 Self-Publishing Success Stories, and
    Lessons You Can Learn from Them			277

Conclusion			287
Endnotes			289

SAM **PEARCE**

Introduction

Welcome to **Book Boss:** *Musings from a Self-Publisher on How to Write, Publish and Market Your Own Book*. If you're a business owner, thought leader or coach looking to share your expertise and build your brand, self-publishing can be a powerful tool in your marketing arsenal. In this book, we'll explore the ins and outs of self-publishing, from writing and design to publishing and marketing, so that you can create a book that not only showcases your knowledge but also helps you connect with your audience and grow your business.

When it comes to self-publishing, there's often a lot of misinformation and confusion out there. That's why we'll start by tackling some of the most common roadblocks that prevent people from becoming authors in the first place. We'll look at the most important questions to ask yourself as an author, how to find the courage to tell your personal story, and how to build an ideal reader avatar that helps you write for your target audience. We'll also dive into the nitty-gritty of writing, from creating a publishing plan to finding the time to write, even with a busy schedule.

But writing is just the first step. To create a book that stands out in a crowded market, you also need to pay attention to design. We'll discuss why cheap design can hurt your book's chances, and we'll share book design secrets from a professional designer. We'll look at common book design mistakes and how to avoid them, and we'll explore the science of how we read and how to use that knowledge to build a better book. We'll also cover the importance of font choice, share our top 10 favourite fonts for books, and give you some tips on manuscript formatting to save time when typesetting your book.

Once you have a great manuscript and a killer design, it's time to publish your book. We'll discuss the pros and cons of traditional publishing versus self-publishing, and we'll explore common self-publishing mistakes and how to avoid them. We'll also cover the practical aspects of self-publishing, from book metadata to ISBNs to book distribution. And because marketing is such a crucial part of self-publishing success, we'll dive into the world of authorpreneurship, exploring how self-publishing can boost your credibility, expand your reach, and help you grow your business.

Self-publishing is an exciting and empowering way to share your knowledge and build your brand. And with the right guidance and resources, anyone can become a successful self-published author. So let's get started on your journey to becoming a Book Boss!

Part 1: ...on Writing

5 Common Roadblocks to Becoming an Author & How to Overcome Them

As we start 2021, becoming an author may be a goal for many of you. But if you're not used to long-form writing, then you may find yourself getting stuck before you've even started. In this article, I want to look at some of the common roadblocks many people face on their journey to becoming an author and give you some advice on how you can overcome them.

Roadblock #1: Time

As business owners, coaches and thought leaders, time is something that we all feel we don't have enough of. So naturally time is one of the most common roadblocks to starting and completing any large-scale project.

I'm not going to lie to you, writing a book takes time; and writing a quality book that will benefit your audience takes even longer. Don't be fooled by these millionaire author courses floating around social media saying that you can write an Amazon bestseller in a weekend. But at the same time, it doesn't need to take as long as you might think… you just need to do a little bit of planning.

Start with writing a book plan. This plan will help you to answer 6 key questions about your book: Who, What, Where, Why, How and When. To find out more about how to write a book plan, see my article "How a Publishing Plan Helped Me Publish a Great Book". You then move on to sketching out a book skeleton, which is a breakdown of the chapters and headings your book is going to contain. You can find out more about how to generate a book skeleton in my article "How I Wrote My Book with Just 30mins a Day". Now that you have your plan and your skeleton, it's time to start writing… but the key is to write regularly and consistently.

A good tip is to look at your existing schedule and find patterns of time where you can fit writing time into regularly. For me, it was my morning coffee. With a little adjustment to my regular routine, I was able to set aside 30 minutes every day to dedicate to writing. Using that process, I was able to finish the manuscript for my first book within 12 months, and the first draft of my second book (which was 50% longer) in just 9 months.

It's important to note that this tip only works if you are consistent. Aim to not skip any more than one or two writing sessions in a row. The more sessions you skip the less momentum you will have and the more progress you will lose. This can easily lead to feeling discouraged and eventually giving up altogether.

Roadblock #2: Imposter Syndrome

Feeling like a fraud is a phenomenon that plagues many successful people. Nearly every writer in history has experienced it in some form or another – including myself. Before I wrote my first book "Stress-Free Self-Publishing", I found myself constantly thinking: "Who am I to write a book on self-publishing – I've only been doing it for 5 years; I'm not an expert". And as a result, I putting it off.

What makes imposter syndrome so common is something called "pluralistic ignorance", which means while we are each second-guessing ourselves privately, we believe we are alone in our doubts because no one else voices their own feelings of doubt. It leaves many of us feeling as though we haven't earned our success, or that our thoughts aren't worthy of attention. This feeling is often intensified by the belief that we are the only ones who feel this way, and in extreme cases, it can even prevent us from sharing ideas, starting that new venture, pursuing certain jobs, or… you guessed it… writing that book.

The good news is that there are 5 simple steps to overcoming imposter syndrome:

1. **Start a conversation.** Confide about how you feel to someone you trust and ask for their opinion/feedback. Often learning that others have experienced similar feelings helps
2. **Own your successes.** We're very good at downplaying our achievements and concentrating on what we could have done better. Instead, start focussing on the positive and listen out for and TRULY hear when someone pays you a compliment. It also really helps to list out your accomplishments; seeing it in black and white can help make it feel more real.
3. **Think in the third person.** British culture is synonymous with the 'reserved stiff upper lip'; celebrating wins is much more of an American thing. If you struggle with step 2, try thinking about those successes as if they were someone else's.
4. **Understand your strengths & weaknesses.** Become more aware of your strengths & weaknesses. If you're not sure what they are, try conducting a SWOT analysis on yourself. Doing this allows you to stop worrying about what you might not be good at and concentrate on what you ARE good at.
5. **Overcome perfectionism.** No one is perfect. Learn to set yourself realistic, challenging yet achievable goals. Start seeing any mistakes you make as a learning experience.

I'm going to leave you with one last thought regarding imposter syndrome, and that is a quote from my coach and mentor Brad Burton who says:

> *"An expert is someone who has made all the mistakes in a given field".*

Roadblock #3: Strategy

This roadblock catches a lot of people out, even experienced authors. They make the mistake of jumping straight into writing a book without first taking a step back to consider how that book fits into the wider picture of their business or personal goals.

Great books do not exist in a vacuum; they serve a purpose not only to the reader but also to the author. Without being clear on what both of those purposes are for your book, the reader will likely forget about you after they've read it, and you will start to forget about marketing it once the initial buzz of launch has faded away.

I touched on this briefly in my tip for overcoming roadblock #1 by answering the Why question in your book plan, but knowing the why is only part of the solution. You need to leverage both your why and your readers' why into a long-term plan of what you want to do with your book once it's published, and what you want your readers to do once they have finished reading it.

A great resource for exploring some of the options of how to leverage a business book as part of a wider strategy is my article "5 Ways a Book Can Boost Your Credibility".

Roadblock #4: What to write about

A statement I hear quite often from people when I explain what I do at SWATT Books is "I'd love to write a book, but I have no idea what to write about".

When it comes to business people wanting to write a book to support their business or advance their careers, this dilemma often stems from too much choice of what to write about as opposed to a lack of ideas.

This can sometimes lead a writer to try and shoehorn everything into one book which results in a book that doesn't have a very clear message or purpose for the reader. If this sounds familiar, check out this article from my good friend Karen Williams from Librotas Book Mentoring entitled "Are you writing more than one book?". Not only is it a great resource to help sort out if you are trying to write multiple books, but it's also a fantastic resource about the different types of business books you could write if you are stuck for initial ideas.

Another aspect of the 'what to write about' roadblock is overlooking what you *could* write about. As an expert in your particular industry or niche, there is probably a lot of useful and informative stuff that you know that you completely forget about simply because it is second nature to you. What might be very complex or confusing to your reader is intuitive to you because of your experience.

A great method for overcoming this roadblock is to sit down and map out your process step by step. This is especially powerful for service-based businesses such as coaches, therapists, and consultants. You will be surprised at what you actually do for your clients that you just don't think about.

P.S. This exercise also has the added benefit of allowing you to refine and adapt your processes, and help you see any gaps that need filling in or unnecessary steps.

Roadblock #5: Brain Dumping/lack of structure

The final roadblock to becoming an author that I see quite often can also be the most painful one because it usually doesn't manifest itself until the writer has already done a considerable amount of work.

If a writer is unaware of, or skips over, the initial planning steps that I mentioned in my tip for overcoming roadblock #1 it's likely that they will just sit down and start to write. It very well may be that they get a considerable amount of content written and feel a vast sense of achievement when they think they have finished their first draft. But then when they read it back cover to cover in the context of an actual book, or have a family member, friend or colleague review it for them, it just falls flat; or worse yet it comes across as incomplete, inconsistent, or just plain confusing. That feeling of achievement is instantly shattered, and they are left feeling demoralised and that they are wasting their time.

This is the potential result of your book not having a structure.

Structure is very important to not only help you write it but to help your reader navigate through the ideas and content that you are writing about. Without it, your book can end up just meandering along simply following your train of thought, as opposed to logically working towards an end goal or outcome.

If you are not very experienced with long-form writing, it can be challenging to initially learn how to convert an idea into a structured piece of writing, but the good news is that there is plenty of help out there in the form of writing coaches and book mentors who can offer guidance and support in determining the best structure for your book. Two that I would highly recommend are Karen Williams with her "Smart Author System", and Jennifer Jones with her "Entrepreneurs' Writing Club".

I hope you have found those tips useful. Writing and publishing a book can be challenging, but it is very worthwhile. And if you can avoid the common roadblocks that people often experience on the journey to becoming an author, you will be more able to enjoy the experience and get the very most out of it.

The Most Important Question to Ask as an Author

There are many important questions you need to ask yourself as an author, but none is more important or far-reaching as "WHY?".

W h y … three little letters that form one of the most powerful words in the English language. Asking "why" of things gives us clarity, understanding, purpose and direction. When it comes to writing a book, asking "why" can help make the process much easier and give your book a greater chance of being successful.

There are two main areas in which you need to ask yourself "why" when it comes to writing a book: your why, and your readers' why.

Your Why

Asking yourself "Why do you want to write this book?" may sound a little rudimentary and obvious but understanding what your motivations truly are will help you get past obstacles when the going gets tough.

Writing a book simply because other people have told you that you should doesn't always give you enough of a personal incentive to dedicate the time and energy that it requires to write a good quality book. Whereas if you have a driving desire to write a book that comes from within, you are more likely to make the sacrifices and put in the time to see the project through to the end.

I've lost count of the number of people I've spoken to who have started a book (some even starting the same book several times over a few years), who never managed to finish it. When I dig a little deeper into what motivated them to start the book in the first place, and what happened to pull them away from the project, more often than not the response boils down to the motivation for writing the book not being as strong as the motivation of the thing that pulled them away from it (whether it be other commitments, lack of time, frustration, etc.).

Writing a book is hard; seeing a book through to publication is even harder. You have to WANT it to see it through to the end.

Your "why" can be anything, as long as it is something that will personally motivate you. It can be the prestige of being a published author, or it can be the desire to teach or leave a lasting legacy. It can be the financial stability of an additional income, or it can be raising your profile within your industry that sets you apart as that 'go-to' expert. You can even have a "why" that is a combination of multiple different reasons. As long as your reason(s) for wanting to write your book are more powerful than the multitude of reasons for not writing it, you'll ultimately get there in the end.

Your Readers' Why

Sitting down and considering your readers' "why" is usually the one thing that tips a book from being just good to being great! Having the answer to "Why should my readers care that I've written this book?" will ultimately guide most of the decisions that you make regarding your book from its content to title; its cover design to your marketing strategy.

Let's be honest… with the millions of books currently on the market, with thousands more being published every year, it is profoundly unlikely that you are writing about something that no one has ever written about before. You need to be able to give readers a reason to buy your book over any of the other books available to them on a similar subject.

As a species, we humans are fundamentally lazy; we want to save time and energy whenever we can. If you can make things quicker and easier for your readers when they are looking for a book on a particular subject by giving them reasons as to why they should buy your book, they will thank you for it. The earlier on in the process that you think about this (ideally before you even write a single word), the easier things will be for you too.

Knowing what makes your book unique in your genre, knowing what your readers will get out of reading it, and knowing how to then communicate all of that to your readers will fundamentally give your book a much greater chance of being successful. Which in turn will ultimately fulfil YOUR "why".

Finding the Courage to Tell Your Personal Story

We all have a story to tell. Our individual life experiences are as unique as a fingerprint, and sharing those stories and experiences with others draws like-minded people to us and fosters a sense of connection and understanding. It can be a very powerful marketing tool as well; a way of making our businesses more 'human' by revealing the story of its founder and/or its' creation.

The problem is the word "personal". It can be very hard, especially if you're an introvert, to allow the line between professional and personal to blur; to let people in to see the *real* you. It takes a willingness to be vulnerable to pull back the curtain and let the world peek behind the scenes. It was a problem I struggled with constantly throughout the journey of writing and publishing my second book "From Broken to Brave".

I am a profoundly private person. I don't believe in airing my personal life all over social media for the world to see. When I wrote my first book "Stress-Free Self-Publishing", many of my beta readers and even a book writing coach whom I often collaborate with mentioned that there was nothing about me or my journey in it. That was very intentional... after all, in my eyes, this was a 'how-to' book and nothing else. But the seed inevitably was planted. I began to question whether the act of sharing my personal story could potentially help other people.

See, my past is littered with some fairly dark and traumatic experiences. From bullying to depression, drug abuse to suicide, domestic abuse to repeatedly having my world turned upside down by events beyond my control and having to start over. If I could help just one person either learn from my mistakes and avoid making them entirely or find the courage and inspiration to move on from similar experiences and become stronger and braver for it, then surely it was worth the discomfort of sharing my story with the world.

So, the very next day after "Stress-Free Self-Publishing" went on sale, I started writing "From Broken to Brave". And it has been such an amazing, cathartic and therapeutic experience, I don't know why I avoided it for so long! I have had some overwhelming responses from people who have read it, that my initial fears of "what will people think of me once they know the truth?" now seem foolish.

If you are toying with the idea of sharing your personal story, but are struggling to find the courage, I want to share some tips with you that I learned along my "From Broken to Brave" journey that might help…

1. Find Your Why

If you're an introvert, or even just a little bit shy, then the idea of sharing your personal story so that people can get to know you better is not enough of an incentive to push past the discomfort and fear of opening up. You need to find a reason that is *stronger* than your fear.

For me, that reason was wanting to help other people either avoid the terrible situations that I found myself in or recover from similar experiences and find their new brave. Making the reason all about them and not me was enough to motivate me past my fears of being judged.

2. Build a Support Network

Pushing yourself far outside your comfort zone is a scary thing, but something that you do not need to do alone. Find one or two people whom you can trust implicitly to be your support network. Let them in on what you are doing and why. Maybe even give them a bit of an insight into the story that you will be sharing. These close confidants can then act as both sounding boards for your ideas and shoulder to lean on when things get tough.

My support network for writing "From Broken to Brave" consisted of my best friend from Canada and my best friend from the UK. That's it, but that's all I needed. Those two people knew most of the story that I was planning on sharing and were able to support me when things got difficult and questioned why I was mentally putting myself through everything again.

3. Create a Safe Space

Writing your personal story, especially if there are any darker aspects to your past, can be a highly emotional undertaking. Quite often reliving past events can bring up long-forgotten feelings that might even go so far as to affect your behaviour for a while. You need to make sure that those around you, particularly your family, know what your plans are and what additional support from them you might need during the process.

Also, consider where you write. Make sure that is a space where you feel comfortable, relaxed and won't be disturbed. It's also helpful, especially if you are going to be recounting particularly traumatic experiences, that you have tokens or mementoes nearby that remind you of positive memories.

Although my husband only knew bits and pieces of the story that I was planning on sharing in my book, I made sure to tell him exactly what I was planning and why I was doing it. I explained that there was a potential for me to get caught up again in what I was writing and that I might need his help to get through it, even though he didn't know the whole story. Thankfully my experience with writing "From Broken to Brave" didn't get as difficult as I initially thought it would, but the odd few times that I did get a bit emotional for no apparent outside reason, he understood and was able to be there for me in the way that I needed.

4. Mentally Prepare for the Reaction

Our lives do not happen in a vacuum; events and experiences in our lives touch and are touched by others around us. You need to be mindful of how your story may affect others; either those directly mentioned in your story, loved ones who may not have been aware of the circumstances at the time of the story, and those closest to you now who may not know about these events at all. Be prepared to have some potentially difficult conversations with people either during the process or after your story is public.

I'm not going to beat around the bush… some of these conversations may be very hard, and as an introvert, you may be tempted to avoid having them. But they are worth enduring because they will inevitably help both you and them to process.

When I decided to write "From Broken to Brave" I knew straight away that I was going to have to have a potentially difficult conversation with my parents. So much of my story that I was planning on sharing in the book I had never told them about or openly discussed with them. I knew that there were going to be feelings of shock, disappointment and hurt once they realised just how much I had kept them in the dark all these years. I had numerous conversations with my mother during the writing process; preparing her for what she was going to learn when I sent her the draft manuscript. We then had a long talk after she had read it so that we could clear the air.

5. Take Care of Yourself

My fifth and final tip is to make sure you take of yourself during this process. Writing your personal story can be an emotionally charged and stressful undertaking, so you need to pay extra attention to your mental, emotional and physical health.

- Get plenty of sleep and make sure you are eating regularly and healthily.

- Keep checking in with yourself to make sure you not getting overwhelmed or emotionally stressed.
- If parts of the story start to get too difficult, don't avoid them but don't force them either. Little and often will help you get through tough sections faster than if you kept putting them off.
- Recharge your "happy battery" as often as you need to. Make a special point to do things that you enjoy throughout the process; play with your kids, go for walks in nature, spend time with your spouse. Whatever you love doing make time to do them regularly.

All of these tips and suggestions will help give you the resilience and fortitude to get through any difficulties you may experience writing your personal story. They will give you the courage and conviction that your story *deserves* to be told and that you are strong enough to tell it.

5 Questions to Ask Yourself When Building Your Ideal Reader Avatar

Before we jump straight into the deep end, let's take a moment to look at what an Ideal Reader Avatar is. If you want to write a successful book, regardless of its genre, the most important thing that you need to know before you pen a single word is… Who Am I Writing This For?

All the important questions you will face whilst writing, publishing and marketing your book will come back to who your reader is. For example

- What language do you use that will speak to them?
- How do you publish your book so they can buy it?
- Where do you market it so they will hear about it?

This is where the Ideal Reader Avatar comes into play, and why it is so vital to the success or failure of your book. It is a profile of your perfect reader that looks at every facet of their lives so that you know the answers to those questions and many more when they come up along your publishing journey.

So, what goes into building a great Ideal Reader Avatar?

Focus

First of all, you need to relieve yourself of one massive misconception right from the very start… your book is not for everyone! Once you realise that, you can start to focus on who your book IS for. Counter-intuitively, the more specific you are the better your book will be for it. Don't be afraid to narrow your focus down to a readership of one – the one single person who would be your ideal reader.

Now, I know what you might be thinking… "If I narrow my focus down that far, am I not excluding all the hundreds or thousands of other readers whom I want to read my book?" Trust me, you're not. Nothing you say or do will *prevent* anyone from buying your book, reading it, or even enjoying it. But what you are doing is making sure that the people who you want to benefit the most from your book, go away from reading it thinking "Wow, that book was amazing… it's almost like they had written it just for me". That is how you create raving fans.

Now that you know we're talking about a single individual, what sorts of things do you need to know about that person to build an Ideal Reader Avatar?

1. Who Are They?

Let's start with the basics and categorize the general demographics of your ideal reader.

- Are they male or female?
- What age are they?
- Where do they live?
- What level of education have they achieved?
- What sort of job do they have?
- How much money do they earn?
- Are they married?
- Do they have children?
- If so, how old are they?

Many successful authors whom I have worked with even go so far as to give their Ideal Reader Avatar a name and find a photograph online that in their mind represents who that person truly is. As we all know, knowing a name and then being able to put a face to that name makes a person real.

Once you know the answers to these fundamental questions you will be able to get into their mindset which will allow you to answer more complex questions about them.

2. Where do they hang out?

Now that you know a little about your idea reader, you can start to dig a little deeper to find out more about them. Specifically, where do they hang out? I suggest looking at this question from all different angles and not just the obvious.

- Where do they spend most of their time?
- What sorts of magazines/newspapers/blogs do they read?
- Who are their friends?
- What do they do for relaxation?
- What sorts of books/TV shows/movies do they like?

Knowing these sorts of things about your ideal readers helps primarily with the logistics of your book. How to publish it; where to sell it; where to market it; and how to structure your marketing so that it speaks to them.

3. What motivates them?

When you know what someone's motivations are, then you can tap into those motivations to not only influence a buying decision but to also elicit a desired response from reading your book. Using the things you know about your ideal reader from the questions above, ask yourself:

- What are the driving forces in their life?
- Are they driven by money or material possessions?
- Are they focused on their family?
- Are they altruistic, and motivated by helping others?
- Are they lacking in confidence and therefore influenced by the opinions of others?

Knowing what truly motivates someone can be a very powerful tool to ensure that your book speaks to that person on a more personal level. It can be the difference between thinking that a book is good and feeling that it was written just for them – that you (the author) truly understand them.

4. What problem does your book solve for them?

If you're writing a fiction book, don't skip past this question thinking it doesn't apply to you… it does – just as much as it does for a non-fiction business book. The core of this question is simply what is the **purpose** of your book? Is it meant to:

- Teach an idea or theory?
- Help them overcome an obstacle?
- Illicit a particular emotional response such as trust or empathy?
- Provide an escape?

If you don't know the purpose of your book, and how that purpose relates to your ideal reader, then how can you know if your book ever fulfils that purpose? The answers to this question, combined with the answers to the next question, also help to form the basis for your marketing message.

5. Why should they care?

The final questions you need to ask yourself about your reader are not only the most difficult to answer but are also some of the most important.

- Why should they care?
- Why should they buy your book instead of another on the same subject?
- Why does it even matter to them that you have written this book?

If you can't answer these sorts of questions as your ideal reader, then how do you expect to convince them to spend money to buy your book and then invest time in reading it?

So, there you have it, the five core questions I use to build an Ideal Reader Avatar. Once you have this avatar planned out, any problem, obstacle or roadblock that crops up during the writing, publishing or marketing of your book will most likely find its solution in these answers. Always reflect any decision you have to make regarding your book back to how it relates to your ideal reader and your chances of publishing a successful book increase exponentially.

How a Publishing Plan Helped Me Publish a Great Book

Amid the Coronavirus Lockdown (May 23rd, 2021 to be precise), my book "Stress-Free Self-Publishing" marked its 1st anniversary. With all the uncertainty and chaos going on at the time I didn't get a chance to properly celebrate my book's birthday, but it did give me a chance to reflect on how it had impacted both my life and my business since its release.

Some of the knock-on effects from publishing "Stress-Free Self-Publishing" were immediately obvious; like the 300% growth of my business that it generated within the first three months of being on sale. Other effects, like the raising of my profile as a credible expert in professional self-publishing, took time to gain momentum but now not a week goes by that I'm not tagged in a post on social media from an author looking for advice or guidance on self-publish.

But my book, like so many others, did not have an easy start. I struggled to get to the point where I had what I felt was a credible book to publish. I couldn't find time to write; I struggled with motivation; I battled with feelings of imposter syndrome, and constantly worried that I was wasting my time. It's a problem I see many first-time authors struggle with too. The turning point for me was the simple, yet highly effective, task of writing up a publishing plan and I recommend every author do it before they write a single word of their book regardless of what publishing route they plan to take.

A Publishing Plan is a combination of three very important and deceptively simple documents: a book business plan, an ideal reader avatar, and a book skeleton. Each document on its own is fairly easy to generate with a little bit of thought, but when combined will answer pretty much any question that might arise during your writing and publishing journey and help you overcome the numerous obstacles that will inevitably crop up along the way.

Let's take a quick look at each part individually:

Book Business Plan

I've already written an extensive article on how to write an effective book business plan, which you can find here. But to summarise, a great business plan aims to answer 6 fundamental questions about your book.

1. **Who** is your target audience?
2. **What** is the key message that you want your readers to get from your book?
3. **Where** does your book need to be available to reach your audience?
4. **Why** are you writing this book, and why should your readers care?
5. **How** are you going to write/publish/pay for your book?
6. **When** do you want your book to be finished and on sale?

By answering these six questions, you are in effect treating your book in the same way that you would treat a business. The answers that you generate from these questions will form the basis for your marketing plan, a realistic budget, and a strategy for getting your book finished and into the hands of your readers.

Some of these questions will require a little bit of research, but I assure you that it is worth putting the time in now to do that research as opposed to getting stuck halfway through and losing momentum.

Ideal Reader Avatar

I always recommend authors generate a separate Ideal Reader Avatar document when working on the Who question of the Book Business

Plan. It ensures that you get to know your reader inside and out. What motivates them? What are their pain points? What problems do they have that you can solve for them? Where do they hang out? What other books/magazines/blogs do they already read?

The more you know about your reader, the more you can write specifically for them. By tailoring your language to them specifically, they will go away from reading your book with the feeling that you were speaking directly to them, and not in a broader general way.

It also helps you to focus your marketing efforts and use language and messaging that will resonate with your ideal reader and motivate them to act and buy your book. If you already know where they hang out, then you know where you should target your marketing efforts as opposed to using a less reliable scattergun method.

Another great byproduct of getting to know your ideal reader is that your book becomes less about you and more about servicing other people. When you are struggling for motivation, this can often be the catalyst that motivates you into action. It becomes harder to ignore deadlines when they aren't just arbitrary dates that you have picked out of thin air but are tied to being required to help your potential clients.

Again, I have an extensive blog article that I wrote on the topic of Ideal Reader Avatars and the sorts of questions you need to ask yourself to flesh out who your reader is. You can read that article here.

Book Skeleton

The final document that you need as part of your Publishing Plan is a Book Skeleton. This is an offshoot of the What question from the Book Business Plan and is probably the one document out of the three that will help you the most initially. It takes the question of *what is the key message that you want your readers to get from your book* and expands it into a list of chapters and headings that will allow you to just sit and write and not have to worry about *what* to write about.

The process of putting together a Book Skeleton is very straightforward. You start with the answer to the question "What is the key message that you want your readers to get from your book" from your Book Business Plan. That is the overarching theme of the book.

You then break that down into sections. Think about the different aspects of your main theme that you could talk about. For example, in "Stress-Free Self-Publishing" my overarching theme is helping authors to self-publish professionally. I broke that down into sections like Before You Start, Editing, Book Design, the Publishing Process, and Marketing. Each of those sections then became a chapter in the book; sometimes with different titles but the content was the same.

I always recommend taking things one step further and breaking each chapter down into different subsections, and these then become the main headings within each chapter. For example, with the Editing chapter in "Stress-Free Self-Publishing" I broke it down to Why editing is important, Different types of editing, Why hire a professional, How you can help your editor, and a bit about Peer Review.

Doing this process and working out in advance what you're going to write about, makes the process of actually writing the manuscript so much easier. You never have to worry about blank page syndrome or writer's block, because you a simply filling in the blanks from your Book Skeleton.

It also makes the issue of finding time to write a bit of a non-starter. Because you already know what you are going to write, you can make use of much smaller blocks of time. With "Stress-Free Self-Publishing" and my upcoming book "From Broken to Brave" I was able to effectively use just 30 minutes each day to write. I would sit down with my morning coffee before going into my office or checking my emails and I would look through my Book Skeleton to select a single heading that I felt motivated to write about at that particular time. I would write on that one topic and then stop to go about the rest of my day. On the days that I just was not motivated to write, I would read through already written sections and make notes of what could be improved when it came time to do my self-edit.

By using this method, you could have the 1st draft of an average non-fiction book (around 12 chapters with 5 headings per chapter) completed in 3 months; and that's without doing any writing on the weekends! No matter how busy your life is, with a bit of planning you can find 30 minutes each day. But I advise that you try to make it the same 30 minutes each day so that your brain starts to associate that time with writing and being creative. If writing doesn't come naturally it will take a bit of time to get used to and build the habit, but the brain is like a muscle that you can train – it just takes perseverance and repetition.

Conclusion

I can hand-on-heart say that without taking the time to work through producing these three documents when I did, "Stress-Free Self-Publishing" would never have been published. I would have remained stuck in the cycle of procrastination, worry, stress and doubt. As a result of thinking about the Who, What, Where, How, Why, and When of my book, "Stress-Free Self-Publishing" has been a phenomenal selling tool for me and an achievement that I am immensely proud of.

By taking the lessons I learned from my first book and writing a Publishing Plan from day one of my second book, "From Broken to Brave", I've been able to go from idea to being on track to publish this coming October in 8 months and with little to none of the stress that I experienced with "Stress-Free Self-Publishing".

Do I encourage every author, regardless of experience or planned publishing route, to take the time and do this one exercise – ideally before you write a single work, but if you have started writing, still do the plan anyway… you'd be surprised at how much easier becomes afterwards.

How I Wrote My Book in Just 30mins a Day

One of the most common questions I hear from first-time authors is "How long does it take to write a book?" Though many experienced authors, writing coaches and publishers can spout all kinds of rough estimates at you, the realistic answer to that question is "How long is a piece of string?" Every book is as unique as the author who writes it. It may take you six months to write a book on the same topic as a book that takes another author two years to write.

In my experience, the reason behind most people asking that question is more of a concern about how much time writing a book may take out of their busy lives. The good news is that with a little bit of planning and habit-building, you can fit writing a book into nearly any schedule no matter how busy you are. In this article, I'm going to share with you some of the tips and processes that I used to get the first draft of my book "Stress-Free Self-Publishing" written using just 30 minutes a day.

Publishing Plan

It all starts with planning… Every good book needs a plan! It doesn't matter what type of book you are writing; fiction, non-fiction, biography, poetry anthology, or children's book you need at least an idea of what you are doing and how you are going to do it before you start.

A book/publishing plan helps you lay the foundations that your book will be built on. It answers the fundamental questions:

- Who is your book for?
- What do you want that reader to get out of it?
- Where are they going to buy it and where are you going to market it?
- When do you want it published?
- How are you going to publish it and who are you going to pay for the support you need?
- Why should your readers care and why do you want to publish this book?

Having the answers to these questions before you start writing will mean that when you do hit those inevitable writer's blocks, you will almost always find the solution somewhere within these answers. The less time you spend trying to solve problems during the writing phase, the faster you'll get the writing done.

If you need help to put together a kick-ass publishing plan, check out this post I wrote on "[How to Write a Publishing Plan](#)", or you can watch the video that the post was based on over on my [YouTube channel](#).

Book Skeleton

Once you've got a basic plan for your book, it's time to start thinking about the actual content that your book is going to contain.

There is no worse feeling for a writer than staring at a blank page for an hour because the words are just not coming. By creating a book skeleton before you start to write your first draft, you will never have to face the dreaded blank page again.

The concept is very simple; a book skeleton is the basic structure of your book. I'm going to illustrate how it works using my first book "Stress-Free Self-Publishing as an example.

You start with the main topic; in this case, "How to Self-Publish a Book". You then break that topic down into a set of broad headings such as

Preparation / Editing / Book Design / Publishing / Marketing – these become your chapters – or at the very least the subjects for each of your chapters if not the actual chapter titles themselves.

Then take each individual 'chapter' and break it down into its various subheadings. So, for example, Book Design breaks down into Why it's important / Benefits of hiring a professional / How to find a professional designer / Outsourced vs DIY / Timing / The design process / eBook conversion / Artwork specifications / etc. Depending on how complex your subject is, you may have to break some of your subheadings down one more level, but that's up to you.

Here is the complete book skeleton for "Stress-Free Self-Publishing" so you can see the concept in action.

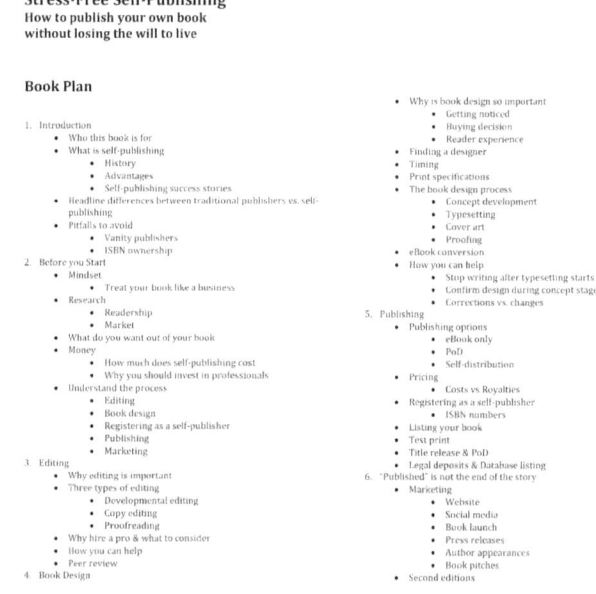

How you go about creating this skeleton is completely your choice. If you're fairly analytical like me, you may prefer to create a bulleted list with varying indent levels to show the structure as in the example above.

Or if you are more of a visual person, you may prefer to use a mindmap approach like this one from Nobleword.

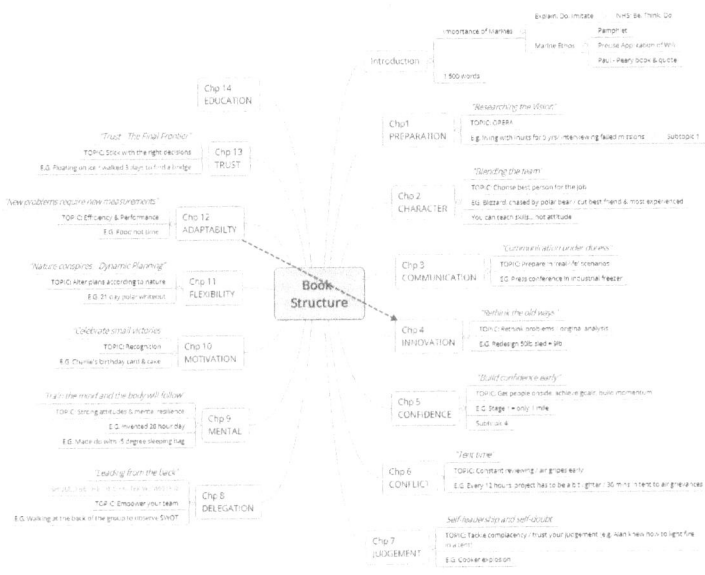

The benefit of using a book skeleton is that instead of opening a blank page and starting to write from scratch, you open your book skeleton and simply pick the subheading that inspires you at that particular moment. It gives you the ability to write your book in a non-linear fashion which helps prevent writer's block, whilst still maintaining your book's structure and flow. Your writing process then becomes about filling in the blanks instead of creating content from thin air.

Fitting in writing time regularly

Now that you have your plan and your skeleton, it's time to whip out the computer, typewriter, or notebook and start writing. You might be thinking that because you've completed all this planning and prep work, that writing your book will be a walk in the park; and it *CAN* be but only if you commit to doing it every day!

All the most successful writers in history are successful because they treated their writing as a job and committed to doing it every day – whether the muse descended or not. Now I appreciate that not everyone can set aside time to write every single day; the important thing is to ***schedule*** a time to write. The goal is to come up with a well-balanced writing routine that provides you with time to write regularly free from disruption and distractions.

A good tip is to look at your existing schedule and find patterns of time where you can fit writing time into regularly. For me, it was my morning coffee. Normally my weekly diary is a mish-mash of meetings, calls, work blocks and family commitments… on first glance, you'd be hard-pressed to find any patterns at all, let alone regular blocks of time that I could take away from my busy day to write. But without fail, I would have a cup of coffee in the morning. Normally, that cup of coffee was drunk whilst going through emails and finetuning my plan for the day.

With a little adjustment to my routine, I'd fix my diary for the next day in the evening before I switched my computer off at night. The following morning, instead of taking my coffee up to my home office, I'd sit in the living room with my iPad and write with my phone still on do not disturb from the night before. No one noticed that I answered emails 30 minutes later than normal and I found my dedicated writing time. Using that process, I was able to finish the manuscript for my first book within 12 months, and the first draft of my second book within 9 months.

Take a look at your weekly schedule and see if there are any pockets of time that you can repurpose for writing. Because you have a book skeleton to work from, you can make productive use of time pockets as short as 30 minutes!

Be consistent

This is probably the most important tip of all – be consistent! Writing is a skill; it takes time to develop. Keep at it, even if it's difficult in the beginning because the more you do it, the easier it becomes. Sure, life gets in the way sometimes, and something may come up that means you need to skip a writing session. That's OK, try to reschedule it for later in the day if you can but if not pick up where you left off at your next writing session. Aim to not skip any more than one session in a row. The more sessions you skip the less momentum you will have and the more progress you will lose. This can easily lead to feeling discouraged and eventually giving up altogether.

The more you can stick to a writing schedule, the more it becomes habitual. If you are not used to doing a lot of long-form writing, you may find it takes you a while to get into the 'flow'. However, forming the habit of writing at the same time every day (or at least at set times each week), the more your brain will start to associate those times with the need to be creative. Just like going to the gym, the more you do it the easier it gets and the quicker you will find your rhythm.

I trust you have found those tips helpful. Hopefully, you can see that you don't need to lock yourself away for months on end to write a book. With a little bit of planning and perseverance, you can fit writing a book into your existing schedule no matter how busy you are.

How to Write an Amazing Book Publishing Plan

I quite often get approached by people who have an idea for a book but don't know where or how to start. I always refer them to this video of a 4Sight talk I gave back in November 2018 titled "So You Want to Write a Book – Now What?". Everyone has always commented on how useful it is, so I've decided to convert it into a full-blown blog for you guys.

As you know I'm Sam Pearce from SWATT Books, and I help people to publish. In the past 5 years since I've been doing that I have worked with loads and loads of authors – I've been privileged to be involved in the publishing of over 40 titles now – and quite often whenever I speak to a lot of those authors they report that at some point in their journey they've got stuck. Whether it's during the writing phase, whether it's during editing, whether it's during publishing; something has come along that they either didn't know what they were doing, didn't know what was supposed to happen next, or something has come along that's knocked them off track. And because of that, it can make the writing and publishing process a bit daunting, a little bit scary, and people sometimes wonder "Why am I putting myself through this, why am I doing it?"

Today I want to share with you the one biggest thing that will help make the process of writing and publishing a book so much easier, so much more enjoyable, and so much simpler to get through from start to finish. I'm not going to kid you, it is still a lot of work, however, if you do this one thing all that work will be a lot less stressful. And that biggest tip is to **treat your book like a business.**

Book Publishing Plan

We're all business people in this room, we know that when you put time and effort and planning into your business, everything is easier, yeah? Books are no different, and this applies no matter what genre you're writing for. Whether you're writing a book to support your business, whether you're writing a children's book, whether you're writing a novel, writing your biography, memoir, or poetry book; it doesn't matter. This one tip can help anybody publish *any* book.

What I'm going to do is I'm going to run through the basics of what you need to do to plan out your book and treat it like a business. You've probably all seen them online before, the simple one-page business plans. It doesn't need to be anything special; you don't need war and peace, you don't need a big heavy business plan that you would prepare to go to your bank or to get investors. This can be really really simple, and it all falls into answering six really simple questions: Who? What? Where? When? How? and Why? Answer those questions everything else becomes so much easier, so much more straightforward.

Who

So first question: Who? Quite simply, who is your target audience? Who is the main reader that you want to go after? Don't be afraid to laser-focus on this. A lot of people do find this a bit counterintuitive. I fell into this exact same trap when I started my business; I thought that if I laser focus on just those key people, aren't I ignoring all of this other potential business back here? No, you're not. When you're writing a book, and when you publish a book, you're not preventing anybody from buying your book. The reason why you want to focus on your specific target reader is because they're your VIPs; they're the ones that you want to please, the ones you really want to get your message across to. If you know in detail who they are, then you can write for them, you can make sure that your language appeals to them, and you can make sure that your content is targeted specifically to them. You're not preventing anybody else from reading your book, or buying your book, or even enjoying your book. But what you're doing is you're making sure that your VIPs are happy.

I would be as detailed about this as you can be. I know some authors that have even gone so far as to give their ideal reader a name, an avatar, what they do for a living, what's their hobbies, whether are they married, how many kids have they got, where they work; all of these things can help you focus on who you're writing for.

What

The next question: What? What do you want to tell them? What do you want to say? What does your book need to be about? This can help you flesh out what the actual skeleton of your book is going to be. Once you start getting into this question, you start building up what your chapters are going to be, and what your headings within those chapters are going to be. By doing this, once you get to the point of writing, all you are doing is filling in the blanks. It makes it so much easier if you know from the very beginning exactly what your book is going to contain. Makes the process much simpler.

Where

Next question: Where? So, where do you want your book to be available? Where is your target reader, that you now know specifically who they are, where do they shop? Do they prefer to shop online or do they prefer to go into a bookstore and leaf through a book? This also helps you decide where you going to do your marketing. Where do they hang out? Are they social media people or do they prefer face-to-face networking or events?

Answering where also helps you figure out a lot of the logistics in terms of where are you going to market and where you're going to have your book available; which in turn will help you sort out things like distribution contracts.

Why

Next question: Why? This is a really big one! It's the one that a lot of people leave out, and there are two parts to this. The first why is why should your readers care. Why should your readers buy your book as opposed to somebody else's who may have written a book about the same subject? when you bring this back to a business context this is basically your USP. What makes you as an author unique? What makes your book unique compared to other books in your genre or your particular subject? What is going to be that one thing is gonna make your readers think "Yes I definitely need that book."

Why is also *your* why. I'm going to be completely open and honest with you, writing and publishing a book is difficult, there is lots of work involved. There is going to come a point where you hit a speed bump; it happens on any journey. You're gonna come across something that's gonna make you think "Oh, why am I doing this? Why am I putting myself through this?" If you know *why* you're doing it for your own reasons, it makes it just that little bit easier to get over that hump and get through to the end.

Your why can be anything, but it needs to be specific to you. Do you want to raise your profile? Do you want to use this as a business card to promote your business? Do you want to get speaking engagements? Or is it just about money and you want the royalties? That's fine if it is by the way because if you do it properly, you can earn money from self-publishing. It doesn't matter what the reason is, as long as you *have* a reason, and you know in your head why you're doing it, it's gonna make it so much easier when the going gets tough.

How

The next question is how. How is simply the logistics. How are you going to publish your book? Are you going to go through a literary agent and try to get yourself a traditional publishing deal, or are you going to self-publish? If you self-publish, are you going to go through a publishing platform like Ingram Spark or CreateSpace and publish print-on-demand, or are you going to self-distribute? Knowing that in advance is going to help you prepare along the way.

How are you going to afford it? If you're going to self-publish there are costs involved that you're gonna have to shell out for upfront. If you know in advance what those costs are, then you can start saving for them, start planning for them, making sure that you know where that money's gonna come from, and then also know how long it's going to take to recoup that money back at the end.

Also, how are you going to market it? This basically becomes your marketing plan. Where are you going to market? What's your message going to be? Are you going to pay for marketing or are you going to do free guerrilla marketing? Knowing all of this stuff in advance means you can start marketing it straight away and start building momentum while your book is in production, which can help with pre-sales and launching your book with a bang.

When

And the final question: when? This is a key one that a lot of authors just completely neglect. Writing takes time. You have to give yourself time to write a book well. And knowing how you write is a key step. Is it something that you're just going to build 30-40 minutes a day into your diary? Or do you need time to going, in which case you need to set aside big chunks of time, maybe even taking a writing retreat and taking yourself away on holiday for a couple of days, a weekend, or even a week and just concentrating on absolutely nothing but your book? Knowing how you write, especially if writing doesn't come naturally to you, is going to make this process just that little bit easier so that you're catering to the way you work.

This helps you also work out just a general schedule. It helps you figure out how long it's gonna take you to write a book, so once you start the pre-marketing that I talked about previously, you've got an idea in your head as to roughly when your book is going to be available. There is no point in building interest if people then come to you and say "That sounds fantastic when can I buy?" for you to answer "Oh I don't know". If you've got an idea, even if it's months in advance, you can say "I'm not too sure yet, but I'm aiming for March next year."

Once you've got those questions sorted you can put a schedule together for yourself. If you're like me and you need deadlines to do something and get something done, having a schedule that's got actual concrete dates on it is just gonna make it a little bit easier when the going gets tough and you need that extra incentive. Giving yourself deadlines just incentivizes you to get it done and get it out there.

Conclusion

So putting a plan together helps for a lot of different reasons. It gives you clarity, and it gives you focus. Those are the two key things that are going to help you get your book over the finish line. But most importantly having a plan is gonna help you overcome those roadblocks that are going to crop up along your journey and helps you get through it.

And I'm speaking about this completely and totally from experience. I'm in the middle of writing and publishing my book now, hoping it's going to be available about March time but I made the classic mistake of starting my book before I did this. And I got stuck! But I tell you what, as soon I did that publishing plan, all of the blocks went away. It doesn't need to be anything specific. That's the publishing plan for my book. Really really straightforward, just notes scribbled down. The headings are not necessarily the questions that I mentioned, but they answer every single one of those questions.

So, if you were thinking about writing a book, and you've got that question in your head of "Okay what do I do now?" Do this!

Want a little bit of extra help to write your own amazing book publishing plan? Just sign up for our mailing list to get your **FREE** Stress-Free Self-Publishing Publishing Plan template. No SPAM, I promise, just great content and news about the world of self-publishing… and the occasional offer on SWATT Books services, courses, and events ;-)

Part 2: ...on Book Design

Why Cheap Book Design Can Be Bad

In this post we're going to explore the most common reasons why design can be cheap, and why those reasons can be bad for your book.

There are four main reasons why book design can be cheap:

1. The book has been designed out of context
2. The design has been rushed
3. The designer lacks education or experience, or
4. The work is not original

Let's explore each of these points in more detail.

1. Context

Good book design needs to have context to have meaning. It has to relate to your story and your audience to be effective. For that, the designer needs time to research your audience and understand your story or subject you are writing about to be able to make design decisions that are relevant to you. Without that research and understanding, the designer will be working in a vacuum. You may end up with a design that looks pretty, but it won't have any relevance to you beyond the superficial.

This also applies to purchased templates. By their very nature, stock templates have been designed to be as generic as possible to appeal to the widest market. They can have their place in the design process if there are unavoidable time or budget constraints; however for them to be effective, they need to be altered to suit your needs first.

2. Time

We've all heard the phrase "Time is Money", and that holds true for book design as well. Good design takes time. A designer needs time to research, brainstorm, generate ideas, and then refine those ideas into concepts; and that is all before you even see a single proof. After that comes typesetting and amendment time. If a designer quotes really cheaply or you negotiate down design costs too much, more than likely the designer A) will not be able to allocate enough time to do a good job without making a loss; or B) may cut corners and miss out key design phases to stay on budget. The result is a design that at best looks good with no meaning, or worse is inappropriate for what you need, is irrelevant to your book, or just plain ugly.

There is a great infographic that I found years ago that illustrates this point perfectly.

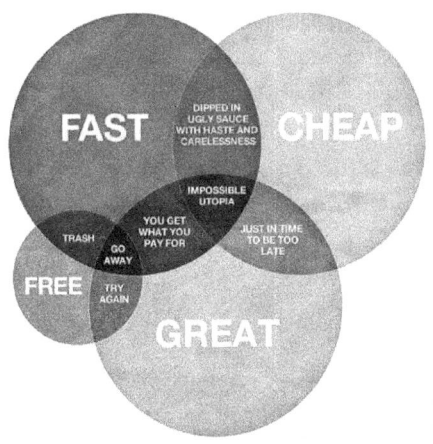

3. Education & Experience

It's a concept that we're all familiar with; the more education and experience you have, the more money you earn. That is doubly true for service-based industries such as design where there isn't a physical product to sell. For designers, our time and our skill IS what we sell, and that skill takes time to learn and years of experience to hone and perfect.

I am not saying that you should not employ the services of an inexperienced designer; how else are they going to get experience? What I am saying is to weigh the decision to utilise a less experienced designer against the complexity of the design you need. Would a less experienced designer be able to produce what you want to the standard of quality you need?

4. Originality

We have already discussed the pitfalls of using purchased templates without adaptation to suit your needs, but there is also the very unpleasant topic of plagiarism, which sadly is all too common in our digital age.

Stolen designs are not only bad for your book for all of the reasons previously mentioned, but it is also downright illegal! As a client, you can run the risk of also being held liable if the IP copyright of a design you have commissioned is challenged. So beware of any designer who cannot or refuses to show you progression work for a design. If you are only presented with polished design concepts (which is a common practice in cover design), you are fully within your right to ask to see sketches or development work for your chosen concept.

Conclusion

There may very well be a utopian designer out there who produces excellent, bespoke design work for next to nothing simply for the love of design. But while you scour the earth looking for them, here are some suggestions on how to avoid the pitfalls of cheap design without breaking the bank:

1. Give your designer as much time as possible to complete a project. Even consider engaging with a designer during the final stages of manuscript editing. A good designer will be able to advise you on ways to approach and manage your book design during the early stages which could save you money in the long run.
2. Think about your design requirements regarding their importance to the saleability of your book. Could the quality of the design mean the difference between making a sale or not? If so, then you should value it accordingly. If not, then it may not require as expensive a solution to meet your needs and something more basic may be sufficient (as long as it is still of a quality and relevance to your audience).
3. Consider the complexity of your book requirements. Does it just need a bit of tidying up? In this case, a more junior/inexperienced designer may be a cost-effective option. However, if it is more complex in nature requiring a more technical design approach and a deeper understanding of book production then it is cheaper in the long run to pay more for a designer with years of experience – you don't want to have to pay extra for it be fixed, or worse completely redesigned, to meet your goals.
4. Lastly, if the money just isn't there to buy the level of service that you need, explore the option of an exchange of services. After all, designers are business people too (though many hate to admit it), and their companies need things just like any other. Maybe you can offer ghostwriting of blog posts for them, or review their website copy? You get what you need without devaluing the services of the designer.

Book Design Secrets from a Professional Book Designer

Many people, authors and readers alike, find it difficult to comprehend just how important book design is to the success or failure of a book. This is because a really good book design is virtually invisible. It blends seamlessly with the content of a book and makes the experience of reading it as effortless as possible. However, most authors have no expertise in book design or typography. As a result, the artwork generation aspect of self-publishing can potentially be very stressful. So, I want to pass on some simple advice to make the process a little easier.

You generally have two options in how you go about generating the artwork for your book, depending on the available budget: hire a professional or do it yourself. Let's look at the pros and cons of each one, and how you can make the most of each option.

Hire a professional

Hiring a professional book designer is by far the best option if you want to publish a good-quality book. There are so many aspects that need to be considered and so many complex decisions that need to be made to get the book design right, which means this option is more than worth the investment. However, it is a considerable investment – the cost to design and typeset a 50k word book can be in the region of £2k-£3k.

If you decide to choose this option, you need to find a designer that specialises in book design. This should be to the point that books are the only type of design work they do. This will ensure that they are 100% familiar with the requirements unique to book design. If you can't afford to work with a dedicated book designer, a more general graphic designer may be more affordable but be sure that at the very least they have experience in designing for print.

Next, you want to have an initial conversation with them. Find out how they work, what their process is, and what sorts of books they have worked on in the past. If you're happy with the outcome of that conversation, ask them to put together a proposal and be sure to read it carefully once it arrives. Familiarise yourself with factors such as how many revisions are included, who will own the rights to the finished design, payment terms and what the likelihood is of incurring extra costs, such as the purchase of stock images or fonts.

By hiring a professional, you can relax and enjoy the design process, safe in the knowledge that you are in capable hands.

DIY

If there isn't sufficient budget in the pot to hire someone to undertake the work for you, then it is perfectly possible to create a quality book by formatting it yourself. This is the cheaper option, but don't forget to factor in the cost of the time required to learn the process and to do the work yourself.

My biggest piece of advice for the DIYers is consistency! Be consistent in your formatting, from start to finish. Make use of the stylesheets feature in programs such as Word, Publisher or Pages, and stylesheet everything! Also, take some time to look through other books that you like, and notice how they have been formatted. This will give you some great ideas for ways of treating different types of content.

Most importantly, don't make it too complicated. Keep the number of fonts you use to a maximum of two or three; avoid having images or graphics which bleed off the page, and work from the starting point of using black and white only. If you're needing to save money with a DIY approach, adding colour to the content and design of your book will add significantly to its cost.

Despite common perception, self-publishing does not mean that you need to do everything by yourself. There is a huge pool of author services available to help you through every step of the process and to offer advice and guidance, even if you want to do the work yourself. Do your homework and make use of the resources available to you; both you and your book will be more successful as a result.

Book Formatting Faux-Pas: 13 Common Typesetting Mistakes

Self-publishing has transformed the book industry, making it possible for anyone to create, publish and sell a book without using a commercial publisher. However, the quality of many self-published books leaves a lot to be desired, and as a result, only a small percentage of self-published books sell in any quantity.

The formatting of your book will play a major part in whether it will be successful or not because it affects both visual appeal and readability. Sadly, many self-publishers fall into the trap of making all too common book-formatting mistakes because they have no formal graphic design training.

As a professional graphic designer, my purpose in writing this article is to make you aware of thirteen easily avoidable formatting errors so that, if you do decide to go down the DIY route, you can still create a book that you can be proud of. Along the way, I'll try and demystify many of the important typesetting terms that can be so confusing. Understanding these expressions will help you should you decide to work with a professional designer.

1. Too many fonts

Today the internet is awash with a bewildering choice of fonts. Microsoft Word comes with almost 50 fonts pre-installed, and Google Fonts offer more than 800 different fonts which can be downloaded for free, and that is just the tip of the iceberg.

Too many fonts can make a layout look amateur, just like THIS.

As a result of all these choices, it can be tempting to use multiple fonts within your book in an attempting be creative or quirky. Don't – it just makes your work look amateurish, reduces your credibility, and makes your book harder to read.

Recommendations:

I would recommend limiting your font usage to two or three. This will give your book consistency and a more coherent look. I'll go more into how to choose those fonts later in this article.

2. Not enough/too much leading

Leading (pronounced "ledding") is the term professional typographers use to describe the spacing between lines of text. The name is derived from the lead shims that were once inserted between rows of movable typeset characters before the advent of digital printing.

Good
Lorem ipsum dolor sit amet, consectetur adipiscing elit. Integer posuere orci quis ligula. Donec egestas massa vulputate nisl. Curabitur venenatis. Nullam egestas facilisis ante. Suspendisse tincidunt. Etiam vitae leo id mauris laoreet luctus. Cum sociis natoque penatibus et magnis dis parturient montes.

Too Little
Lorem ipsum dolor sit amet, consectetur adipiscing elit. Integer posuere orci quis ligula. Donec egestas massa vulputate nisl. Curabitur venenatis. Nullam egestas facilisis ante. Suspendisse tincidunt. Etiam vitae leo id mauris laoreet luctus. Cum sociis natoque penatibus et magnis dis parturient montes.

Too Much
Lorem ipsum dolor sit amet, consectetur adipiscing elit. Integer posuere orci quis ligula. Donec egestas massa vulputate nisl. Curabitur venenatis. Nullam egestas facilisis ante. Suspendisse sociis natoque penatibus et magnis dis parturient montes.

Most word processing programmes will refer to it simply as "line spacing" and allow you to choose from a limited range of preset values such as 1, 1.5 or 2. Professional typesetting software such as Adobe InDesign allows a much finer level of control over leading.

Why is leading important?

The spacing between lines impacts the readability and mood of your text. Tight leading usually makes the text harder to read while creating a more tense and intimidating feel.

Leading that is too big also makes the text harder to read because the sentences lose their connection and the reader's eye does not flow naturally from one line to the next.

Recommendations:

Manuscripts are usually created double-spaced because: a) it makes them easier to read and b) the extra space allows editors to write comments above the text.

However, when it comes to typesetting your book for printing, I recommend that you reduce the leading to a maximum of 50%—i.e.1.5 times the size of your chosen typeface. For example, if you are using 10 point type, I would suggest using 14 to 15-point leading.

4. Widows & Orphans

The terms Widows and Orphans, in a typographic context, relate to single words or short lines of text which are left hanging at either the top of a page or the end of a paragraph.

A "widow" is a paragraph-ending line that consists of a single word or the end of a hyphenated word, thus leaving too much white space before the next paragraph.

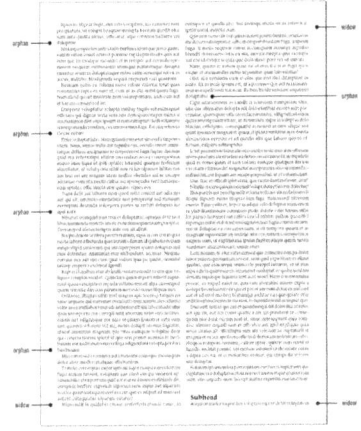

An "orphan" is a paragraph-ending line that appears by itself at the top of a page or column, and is thus separated from the remainder of the associated text.

Recommendations

Leave fixing widows and orphans until last as any changes to the text, font, leading, etc. will affect the occurrence of these stylistic anomalies.

Ways to eliminate widows	Ways to eliminate orphans
• Adjust the horizontal spacing between words • Adjusting the hyphenation of words • Rewording the paragraph	• Force a page break early • Adding or resizing figures to make the text fit the space

Microsoft Word does have automated widow/orphan control (which you can find under Format > Paragraph > Line and Page Breaks. I suggest not to use it blindly. Even if you have the feature turned on, manually review your manuscript line by line once you are ready to print to make sure that no instances have slipped through.

5. Mismatched alignment

By this point in the article, you can't have missed the importance of consistency when it comes to formatting your book. Alignment is yet another area that self-publishers often slip up on unless they get professional help.

What do I mean by Alignment?

Alignment relates to the way the text in a paragraph is aligned. Most word processing programmes offer a choice of four standard alignments:

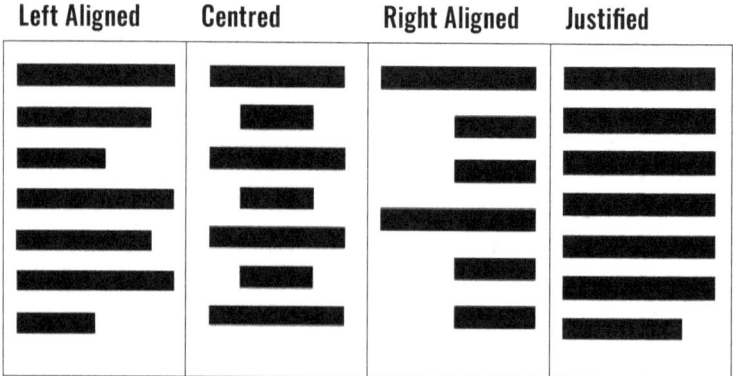

Left Aligned   Centred   Right Aligned   Justified

Recommendations

Avoid using multiple alignment settings as this will make your book look messy and unprofessional.

Only use justified alignment with hyphenation turned ON, and use good hyphenation techniques (i.e. setting minimum word lengths, the maximum number of hyphenations per paragraph, etc.). This will allow you to control the inconsistent spacing that occurs in the middle of lines with justified text (also known as text "rivers").

6. Using an unsuitable font

With so many fonts available today it's no surprise that many authors resort to the default fonts suggested by their word processor. While these are a "safe bet", they limit your ability to match your font to the nature and tone of your book. In so doing, it can reduce your books' impact.

Some examples of unsuitable fonts for book use

Courier	Not proportional so will make your text look messy
Times New Roman	It's the default for many word processors and so doesn't stand out
Bodoni	Its high contrast makes it unsuitable for large blocks of small text
Slabo	Its square serifs make it blunt and unattractive for large text blocks
Arial	Overused and can be boring
Eurostile	A mixed style font that is neither one thing or another
Impact	A thick and heavy font that is too "shouty" for large blocks of text

Recommendation

Choosing the right font is important because it affects both the readability and mood of your book.

As mentioned earlier under the "too many fonts" section, you should limit your font selection to a maximum of three.

Choose your font(s) with care, considering four main criteria: readability, suitability to the subject, relevance to the audience, and aesthetics.

For a more in-depth analysis check out my article on font choice.

7. Ignoring hierarchy

Hierarchy is used in typography to denote the order of importance of different textual elements in your book for example Chapter titles, section headings and body copy.

Heading 1 grabs your attention
Heading 2 helps you find your way
Heading 3 alerts you to subtopics
Heading 4 isn't shouting but won't be ignored
Body text is smaller than all the headings. It'll get your attention by being concise and compelling, but it won't compete with the headings.

As you can see from the (inset) Hierarchy can be established in a variety of ways. Common elements you can use to establish hierarchy include font change, text size, weight (bold, regular, or light), case (uppercase, title casing, or sentence case), spacing, and Contrast. Typically, the most important element is the biggest and boldest with the next most important information presented in a slightly smaller and less dramatic font. This design formula helps readers to scan the page and quickly pick out the most relevant information for their needs.

Recommendations

Missing or inconsistent hierarchy leads to confusion in the reader's mind as they don't know where to begin. If such a structure is appropriate, as is often the case in nonfiction books, establish it early on with an appropriate choice of fonts, styles and sizes and then use it consistently throughout your manuscript.

8. Overuse of emphasis

Emphasising certain words or ideas in your book can help your reader, but many authors tend to get carried away once they start down this road.

There are various ways to emphasise important ideas in your book such as **bold text**, underlining, *italics* and UPPER CASE.

Recommendation

Emphasis should be used sparingly so "less is more" should be your mantra. Also, don't mix several forms of emphasis in the same passage. If your message isn't clear, then consider rewriting it or adding a photograph, chart, or diagram to provide an alternative form of emphasis.

9. Double spacing after the end of a sentence

Typographers use the term sentence spacing to refer to the horizontal space between one sentence and the next. It used to be common practice to add extra spaces after a full stop, but this practice has been phased out in printing since the middle of the 20th Century.

Recommendation
If you look online you will still find arguments about whether one space or two spaces is "correct."

I would recommend that you use single spacing as there is no evidence that it has any detrimental effects, and it is the norm in the publishing industry. So make sure to check your manuscript and eliminate any additional spacing between sentences. If your book is particularly long, you may be pleasantly surprised to find that this trick could even reduce your overall page count.

10. Mismatching fonts

Consider the compatibility of your fonts. Fonts on their own can look great, but not all fonts play well together. It's common to use different fonts for headings subheadings and body text, so it is important that you choose fonts that harmonise well.

THESE FONTS Complement each other	THESE FONTS Don't harmonise well together

Recommendation

When font matching, consider pairing a serif with a sans serif. It doesn't matter which way round you use them (serif for body copy and sans for headers, or vice versa), but the contrast between the two styles will add a level of visual interest to your book and aid in establishing hierarchy.

One fool-proof way to avoid clashing fonts is to choose two different styles of the same font, for example, Freight Sans and Freight Text. These font pairings have been designed to complement each other.

11. Not setting appropriate line lengths

Believe it or not, the number of characters on each line of your printed book has been shown to affect its readability. Lines that are too long cause your readers to have difficulty focusing on the text. Lines that are too short are also difficult to read. The reader's eyes are forced to travel back to the start of the next line more frequently, breaking their natural reading rhythm and resulting in stress and fatigue. Various studies have come up with an optimal line length of between 50 and 75 characters.

Recommendation

Ensure that your book is as readable as possible by limiting your line lengths to between 50 and 75 characters.

For more information read my article about the science of how we read and its implications for book design.

12. Ignoring contrast

Contrast, as its name suggests refers to the difference between elements on a page. For example, the difference in colour between the text and the page background, or the difference between a big bold headline font and a smaller, lighter font used for body text. Research has shown that the image-processing part of our brain likes contrast.

- Contrast is attractive
- Contrast helps us organise information
- Contrast creates a focus

Self-publishing authors who ignore the importance of contrast pay a price, both in terms of poor cover design, and overall readability. Thin grey fonts on a paler grey background may look good but can be hard to read.

Recommendations

Look for ways to add visual contrast to your book, in both cover design and interior formatting. But as with everything, don't overdo it. The best place to start is by ensuring that there is enough contrast between your headings or chapter titles and your body copy.

13. Improper use of punctuation characters

Ask any proofreader what the most common mistake they come across is, and they'll probably say punctuation mistakes, especially the dreaded apostrophe. From a typographer's point of view, there's more to it than correct grammar. Of course, you should check that you are using the correct punctuation for your sentence but also think about HOW you are formatting your punctuation. Here are just some of the elements that a professional typographer will consider:

- The spacing between letters and punctuation characters.
- The use of 'single' and "double" quotation marks
- The position of a full stop (period) or question mark in relation to any associated quotation marks – inside or outside?
- The italicising of full stops, colons, semicolons and question marks if the word preceding them is italicised
- Dash lengths and the spacing before and after them
- The spacing before and after special characters such as © % &

Recommendations

The rules relating to the typesetting of punctuation characters often vary between nationalities. American typesetting rules are different from British English for instance. I recommend that, if you are going to do your own typesetting, do your research on punctuation best practices in your primary marketplace. Once you've settled on a set of 'rules' for how you are going to format your punctuation – apply those rules consistently.

In conclusion

Having read this article, you'll now have a much better awareness of the most common typesetting errors and how to avoid them. You'll also have an appreciation of how these small but important technicalities affect both the readability and credibility of your book.

If you only take two things from this article, I'd like them to be:

1. **That you remember the importance of visual consistency:** The largest part of our brain's information processing capacity is dedicated to sight. This means that even tiny inconsistencies in things like alignment, fonts, line spacing, and hierarchy get noticed, affecting our overall impression of the publication.
2. **To consider the scale of the task:** Ask yourself if you have the time, skill and patience needed to typeset your own book

Given the range of faux pas listed in this article and their potential for damage, wouldn't it make more sense to let a professional like me do it for you?

5 Common Book Design Mistakes & How to Avoid Them

Let's be honest, not every author can afford to have their book designed and typeset by a professional. For those authors on a tighter budget, producing your own book artwork is entirely feasible, but there are some common book design mistakes that you need to be aware of and try to avoid.

In this article, I'm going to look at the 5 most common book design mistakes that I see and give you some tips and advice as to how you can avoid making the same mistakes with your next book.

Book Design Mistake #1: Pagination

If you are producing your book using a word processor like Microsoft Word, it's very easy to lose sight of the fact that a printed book is a three-dimensional object – it has a left and a right-hand page when open. Where your content falls in relation to this left-hand/right-hand layout is referred to as Pagination.

One of the book design mistakes that I see most often is books that don't take this left-hand/right-hand layout into account. It's very easy to spot books that make this mistake; page numbers or headers and footers might move from one page to the next, and margins might shift left or right and then back again.

The good news is that this is an easy mistake to avoid. Here's how:

- Remember that traditionally odd-numbered pages sit on the right-hand side of the spine, and even-numbered pages sit on the left.

- Book content always starts on a right-hand page (even if that first page is not numbered as page 1).
- To make things simple for yourself, align page numbers as well as headers and footers to be centred on the page, ideally between your margins.
- For books of 150 pages or less, you can use the same margins left to right as long as they are at least 9.6mm or more.
- For books of more than 150 pages, you will need to set the inside (that's the one that sits against the spine) to be wider than the outside margin. To do this in Word, go to Format > Document. Select "Book Fold" for the Multiple Pages option under Pages, and then set your Inside and Outside margins accordingly. See below for a table of MINIMUM margin requirements as recommended for Amazon KDP compliance to give you a guide of what margins you should be using.

Document

Margins | Layout

Top:	0.94cm
Bottom:	0.94cm
Inside:	1.27cm
Outside:	0.94cm
Gutter:	0 cm
Gutter Position:	Inside

Pages
Multiple Pages: Book fold
Sheets in booklet: All

Apply to: Whole document

Default... | Page Setup... | Cancel | OK

Page count	Inside (gutter) margins	Outside margins (no bleed)	Outside margins (with bleed)
24 to 150 pages	0.375" (9.6 mm)	at least 0.25" (6.4 mm)	at least 0.375" (9.4 mm)
151 to 300 pages	0.5" (12.7 mm)	at least 0.25" (6.4 mm)	at least 0.375" (9.4 mm)
301 to 500 pages	0.625" (15.9 mm)	at least 0.25" (6.4 mm)	at least 0.375" (9.4 mm)
501 to 700 pages	0.75" (19.1 mm)	at least 0.25" (6.4 mm)	at least 0.375" (9.4 mm)
701 to 828 pages	0.875" (22.3 mm)	at least 0.25" (6.4 mm)	at least 0.375" (9.4 mm)

Book Design Mistake #2: Headers/Footers

The next common book design mistake that I see most often relates to a book's headers and footers. Book headers and footers traditionally consist of the book title, author name, and page number. In non-fiction books, they often also include chapter or section titles to aid readers in navigating through the book.

I quite often see books, where these headers and footers have either not been applied consistently in terms of their content or their location, causing them to shift slightly on the page.

As with Pagination, mistakes with headers and footers are easy to avoid, just follow these simple tips:

- Make use of the Headers/Footers feature in MS Word by double-clicking either the very top or bottom of any page.
- Do not manually type in page numbers; let Word add them automatically by using the page number options inside the Headers/Footers formatting window.
- If you are including chapter/section titles in your headers/footers, be sure to update the Header/Footer content at the start of each chapter or section.

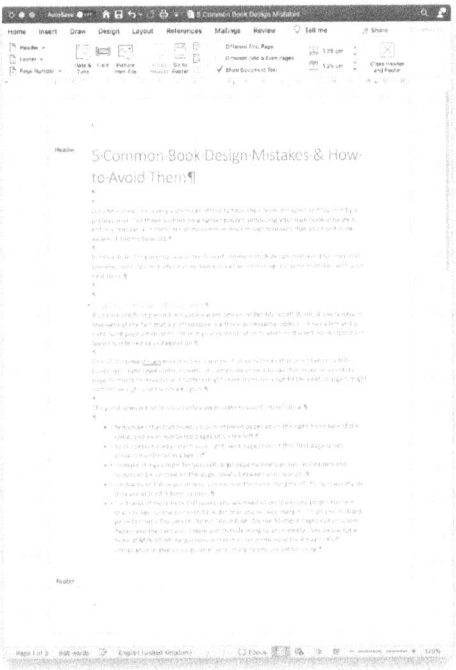

Book Design Mistake #3: Font Choice

This next book design mistake has a couple of different facets to it – one that is straightforward, but one that is a little bit more arbitrary and personal – but they both relate to the choice of fonts that you use to typeset your book.

The more clear-cut mistake regarding font choice is a book that uses too many different fonts and font styles. Books that exhibit this mistake tend to make readers feel a bit confused, overwhelmed or just plain distracted from the content. It makes a book look messy and not very coherent.

The font-related mistake that has a bit more grey area around it is that of the actual fonts you choose and how they relate to the content, purpose, and message of your book. Fonts can have a profound subliminal effect on a reader's interpretation of your message. You can be saying one thing, but your choice of fonts could be giving the complete opposite impression. Take the examples shown right for instance.

I am traditional and conservative

I am modern and forward-thinking

I am fun and light-hearted

I am important and urgent

Avoiding font-related mistakes can be a bit tricky for some, especially if you're not very visually creative, but following these basic guidelines will help:

- Keep the number of fonts that you use to a maximum of 3, but ideally to 2. Then use different weights and styles within those fonts if you want to get more creative.
- Make sure that the two-three fonts that you choose work well together a don't clash. If in doubt, try looking for a 'superfamily' of fonts; these are serif and sans serif fonts created specifically to go together (check out this collection of Superfamilies from Google Fonts).
- Think carefully about your target audience and the message that you want to convey to that audience, then try to select fonts that reflect that message.
- For more guidance on how to choose fonts for your book design, check out my article Why Font Choice is So Important in Book Design.

Book Design Mistake #4: Formatting Consistency

The fourth in my list of book design mistakes is one that tends to send my OCD into overdrive… and that is a lack of consistency in text formatting.

Consistency is king in any type of visual design but is especially important in book design. A lack of consistency can make a book look messy and in the case of non-fiction books can be confusing for the reader. If you start your book formatting quotes in italics with no speech marks, and then later switch to regular text with speech marks, will your reader recognise it as a quote? If they are specifically looking for a quote in your book, they might skim over it because it's not formatted as they expect based on the quotes they saw earlier in the book.

Avoiding making mistakes in the consistency of your formatting is fairly easy to do, but it takes some planning. Here is my recommended workflow to keep your formatting consistent from Introduction to Conclusion:

1. Before you start typesetting your final book, skim through your entire draft manuscript and make a list of the different types of formatting your book will require. Be sure to look at both paragraph and character formatting.
2. Go through your list and decide how you want each formatting style to look. It's best to open a new Word document and format a selection of copy in each style.
3. When you are satisfied with how each style looks both in isolation and in relation to the other styles, save each type of formatting as a Style in Word by opening the Styles Panel accessible from the Home menu at the top of the screen.
4. After saving each formatting style, delete all your formatting text and copy in your draft manuscript. Systematically work through your book page by page formatting the content using ONLY the styles that you saved.

Book Design Mistake #5: Alignment

This final book design mistake is a minor one in the grand scheme of things, but if you can avoid it will make your book look that much more professional; and that is text alignment.

Though there is nothing wrong with left-aligned text, a book where there are pages and pages of text with a ragged right can look messy and could potentially give your reader a headache after a while.

This also applies to your left-hand alignment. If your book contains bullet points, numbered lists, or sections of indented text, you don't want that left-hand alignment changing from page to page. Again, it adds to the messiness and makes it more difficult for the reader to comfortably read your book for extended periods if their eye has to keep shifting to find where new lines start.

This last book design mistake is also a simple one to avoid, just follow these simple guidelines:

- Format all paragraphs of body copy using **Justified** alignment to ensure straight edges on both sides of your text.
- Use a consistent amount of indentation on all bullet points, numbered lists, and indented text.
- And be sure to add that indentation amount to your formatting Styles (as discussed above) to guarantee consistency throughout your book.

Conclusion

I always advocate hiring a professional designer to design and format your book. They will instinctually know how to avoid all these common mistakes and many more that I have not mentioned.

However, if you just do not have the budget to pay for a professional, then following these tips will help you produce a book that is consistent, easily readable, and of a high enough quality that it will be judged on its content and not on how it looks.

If you have any other design and formatting suggestions, I'd love to hear about them. Drop your tips and ideas in the comments below.

The Science of How We Read and How to Use it to Build a Better Book

Scientists and philosophers since the time of the ancient Greeks have been fascinated by the incredible power of the human brain to decode markings into meaningful messages. Researchers have proposed, tested and discarded scores of theories in search of an answer to the apparently not-so-simple question, "How do we read?"

Wait, What Has This Got to Do with My Book?

Understanding the implications of the latest research on this topic can help you design a better book. One that is easier to read, and therefore more likely to sell. Self-published authors who are ignorant of these findings generally suffer:

A. **A loss of impact:** A book that is hard to read will undermine your best endeavours to influence others, diminishing, rather than enhancing, its reach and impact.
B. **Reduced sales:** All other factors being equal, a poorly designed book will sell fewer copies than a well-designed one.

What is the Science of Reading?

There are two core aspects of reading: recognition of individual words and then associating those words together to decipher the context of a passage of text.

Word Recognition:

There are four main theories of how the brain recognises and interprets individual letters into words. Some theories are more robust than others, but all have a level of validity to them.

Theory 1 – Bouma Shape Recognition

The idea that we recognise words by the shape they make was first proposed by psychologist James Cattell in 1886[1].

Subsequent, more rigorous research, published in the late 1960s and early 1970s, supported Cattell's findings, including extensive experimentation by Herman Bauma[2], a Dutch Vision Researcher in 1973.

When letters are combined in words, the pattern of neutral, descending and ascending characters form an overall shape envelope for each word. During his earlier research into the theory, Cattell discovered the 'Word Superiority Effect'[3], which demonstrated that people have better recognition of letters presented within words as compared to isolated letters and to letters presented within nonword strings.

Theory 2 – Serial Letter Recognition

Psychologist Philip Gough proposed an alternative model in 1972 in which he claimed that words were read letter-by-letter from right-to-left[4]. The serial letter recognition theory gained rapid popularity due to its simplicity and testability. It successfully predicted that shorter words are more rapidly recognised than longer ones, however, it couldn't account for Cattell's Word Superiority Effect and was discredited as a result.

Theory 3 – Parallel Letter Recognition

The emergence of technology which allows researchers to track a test subject's eye movements with a high degree of accuracy led to a new theorem known as Parallel Letter Recognition.

The model generally states that the letters within a word are recognised simultaneously, and that letter information is then used to identify words from a library of learned words[5]. This theory has superseded both the shape and serial letter recognition hypotheses and is currently the most widely accepted theory among cognitive psychologists[6].

Theory 4 – Neural Network Model

Recent advances in the science of the way our brain cells (neurones) work have given rise to an even more sophisticated understanding of how we read and process words.

The Neural Network Model proposes that various visual aspects of a word, such as horizontal lines, vertical lines, and curves, trigger word recognition receptors within the reader's brain. Stimulation of these receptors, in turn, excites or inhibits neural pathways to other words in the reader's memory.

Words with a similar visual representation to the observed word receive excitatory signals. Simultaneously, connections to words with a dissimilar appearance receive inhibitory signals. This combination of strengthening links to relevant words, and weakening associations with irrelevant ones, eventually activates the correct word as part of word recognition in the neural network[7].

Research supporting the Neural Network Model was published by neuroscientist Maximillian Riesenhuber, from Georgetown University Medical Centre, in March 2015[8].

Deciphering Context:

We have known since the late 19th century that the eye does not move continuously along a line of text when we read but instead makes short rapid movements (called saccades) intermingled with short stops (called fixations).

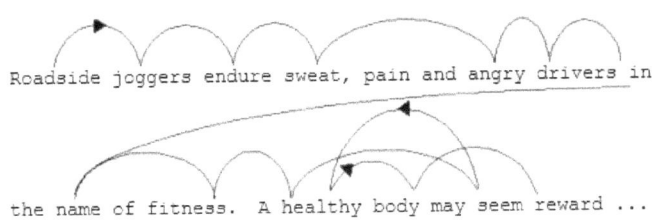

A diagram demonstrating a typical saccadic eye movement

How Saccadic Eye Movement works[9]:

Eye movement studies using sophisticated eye-tracking technology indicate that we use three main areas of visual acuity when reading. The first area is centred on the fixation point and is where word recognition takes place. This area is usually large enough to capture the word being fixated as well as smaller function words directly to the right (such as 'and', 'if', and 'the').

The second zone extends a few letters past the fixation word and is used to gather preliminary information about the next letters in the sequence. The last area extends as far as 10-15 letters past the fixation point and is used to identify both the length of the following words and the best location for the next fixation point.

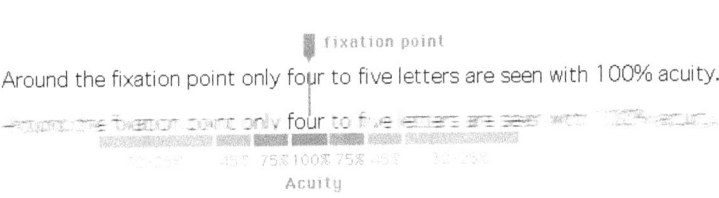

A diagram demonstrating the zones of foveal vision in reading

How Does This Research Relate to Book Design?

In the remainder of this article, I want to drill down into the various elements of book design to see how they relate to topics such as readability and comprehension.

Capitalisation

Research shows that most people read uppercase text 5-10% slower than standard sentence case content. The prevailing theory for this result is that we are not used to blocks of upper-case only text, and so it takes our brain longer to process than lower-case text with occasional capitalisation.

Recommendation:

Use blocks of upper-case text sparingly and ideally not within the body copy of your book. Try to only use it for single words that you wish to add emphasis to by making the reader subconsciously take longer over that word, or for headings.

Font selection

The font you chose can dramatically affect the readability of your text.

Serif versus Sans-serif fonts (Image)

There is much contention in the design world as to whether Serif or Sans Serif fonts are easier to read. However, the latest brain research suggests that, when it comes to readability, there is little solid evidence either way. So, the choice of font classification generally comes down to personal preference, if you are mindful of *how* that font is used (more on that later).

Font design and readability (Image)

The advent of computers and digital typesetting has opened the door to a plethora of modern decorative fonts which, although more stylish, are often harder to read. Did you notice that all the scientific theories discussed above depend to some degree on being able to decipher individual letter characteristics? If the font you choose is so decorative that the letter forms are not immediately clear, it will take the brain longer to decide what each letter is, causing the reader to get fatigued and possibly lose interest.

Recommendation:

Use decorative or display fonts with considerable care, even when setting headings. These typefaces should only be used to add a particular mood or style to your book when that is required. Even then, you need to make sure that the text is still easily legible.

Font readability and perceived task difficulty

Research by Hyunjin Song and Norbert Schwarz of the University of Michigan[11] indicates that the harder a passage is to read, the more challenging the action written about will appear to be to the reader. By testing the reader's reactions to the same set of instructions presented in either an easy or a hard-to-read font, the researchers could show a direct correlation between readability and perceived task difficulty.

Recommendation:
If you want your readers to act after reading your book, it makes sense to choose a simple, highly legible font and set the text with minimal decorative features. This will make the text easier to understand and therefore reduce any subliminal barriers to subsequent application.

Font size

Now, having selected a font that is appropriate and readable you might think that your work is done, but you'd be wrong. The next thing to consider is the size of the font, also referred to as point size. You are probably familiar with the fact that you can change the size of your chosen font simply by selecting an option in the menu of your word processor. But have you stopped to consider what is the ideal font size for the headers, subheaders and body copy in your book?

Clearly, font size has an impact on readability. Why else do you think we have "small print" in most contracts? All other things being equal, the smaller the font size, the harder it is to read. But, on the other hand, the bigger the font, the more pages in your book, and the more expensive it will be to print. Research conducted at the University of Minnesota and the Rochester Institute of Technology[12] suggests that the minimum print size for readability is 9pt. However, it should be noted that the design characteristics of the font used can have an impact on this.

Recommendations:
I would recommend the following font sizes for most books but remember to take your target readership into account when making your final decision.

- Body copy 9-12pt
- Chapter Headings 16+ pt
- Subtitles 12-14pt

Line length and readability

Font selection is not the only thing that affects readability. The number of characters per line (including spaces) has also been found to have a significant impact on legibility.

Research by the Baymard Institute[13] suggests that the ideal line length should be between 50-75 characters. Longer lines are harder to read because it is more difficult for the eye to take in where the line begins and ends. Shorter lines are equally difficult to read because they force the eye to jump around too much, disrupting the reader's usual eye movement pattern, so it is important to strike a balance between the two.

Recommendation:

Make sure that your line lengths are between 50-75 characters. To achieve this, you need to balance several interlinked factors including page size, font, font size and page margins.

The Important of Spacing

The relationship between spacing (both horizontal and vertical) and the legibility of text was brought to the forefront in 2008 when two neuroscientists from New York University published the findings of a study called "The Uncrowded Window of Object Recognition" in the scientific journal Nature Neuroscience[14].

One of the essential elements of spacing in book design is the choice of line spacing, the vertical distance between lines of text in your manuscript (known in the design industry as leading). Research has shown that there is a relationship between font size and line spacing (leading) that directly affects the readability of your book's content. Most sources suggest that a good rule of thumb is to use a line spacing that is between 120 and 135% of the point size of your chosen font.

Recommendation

Based on my experience having designed many successful fiction and nonfiction books, I would recommend using a slightly wider leading than the default leading set by many word processors and page layout programs (in the region of 130% of your font size). For example, 13pt leading on 10pt text. This gives your text more breathing space and makes it easier for the reader's eye to travel from the end of one line to the beginning of the next.

The horizontal spacing between the letters in the same line is the second element that has a significant effect on the legibility of your book. This is known in the design industry as Kerning. When letters appear crowded together on the page, it makes it much harder for the brain to separate and identify the letters and therefore the words that they make up.

Recommendation

The page layout program InDesign (which is the design industry standard for typesetting) has incorporated a function to set your kerning amount to 'Optical' automatically. This applies a mathematical algorithm based on the font used to ensure that there is enough space between each letter to be optically distinguished from its neighbours. This is ideal for large amounts of text; however, every good designer will recommend that titles and main headings be kerned letter-by-letter for the best results.

In Summary

Objective scientific research into how we read has reinforced what professional designers and publishers have known for years. That the typography of a book will have a significant impact on readability and comprehension, which in turn affects sales.

Typography is a combination of art and science. Finding the ideal blend of font, font size, line spacing, and letter spacing takes careful consideration, an understanding of the science of reading, and an artist's eye to be able to blend objective research with the aesthetic.

Why Font Choice is So Important in Book Design

Clearly, writing the manuscript for your book is a critical first step on the road to becoming a published author, but there are other essential elements that you should think about if your book is to be successful. These include editing, interior layout, typesetting, and formatting, as well as cover design.

In this article, I'd like to share some ideas to help you appreciate the importance font choice makes to the overall success of your book.

It may surprise you to know that there are 32,000 font families (typefaces) in existence at the time of writing this article, so it's no wonder that choosing the best one causes many authors so much angst. Thankfully there are some simple criteria that you can use to whittle this bewildering array down to a manageable shortlist. Let's look at each of these criteria in turn and see what it means and how it affects our font choice. But first, a brief introduction to fonts themselves.

Fonts 101

Fonts typically fall into four main categories – Serif, Sans-Serif, Script, and Display. The first fonts used by printers were influenced by the handwriting of the period. Each character was separate but had little flourishes at its edges, called serifs.

In the high-resolution world of printed materials such as books, these serifs make each letter distinctive and therefore easier for our brains to recognise and read. They also help our eyes to flow from one letter to the next binding individual characters into words. One of the most common serif fonts is

Times New Roman, which was commissioned by The Times newspaper in 1931 specifically to improve the readability of its publication.

> Times New Roman
> Garamond
> Palatino
> Warnock Pro

However, this generalisation does not necessarily hold true for digital displays. The lower resolutions of computer monitors, coupled with some of the thinner elements of serif characters can make Serif fonts harder to read on screen.

As a result, a new category of fonts started to appear called Sans-Serif (from the French word "sans" meaning "without"). These fonts had the flourishes removed, and the thickness of each stroke evened out to create letterforms that were more conducive to digital reproduction.

> **Arial**
> Helvetica
> Futura
> **News Gothic**

The introduction of computer typesetting eliminated the need for each letter to be a separate block as was required for traditional letterpress typesetting. And so, it became possible to create Script fonts that more closely emulated the flowing connected letters of handwriting.

Bickham Script
Edwardian Script
Mistral
Snall Roundhand

This new freedom also allowed font designers unlimited creativity when crafting new typefaces and brought about the advent of the final category of fonts; known by various names including Display, Decorative or Novelty. While these decorative fonts certainly stand out, their focus on form over function makes them unsuitable for large blocks of text. They should, therefore, be used sparingly.

ALLSTAR
Curlz
MEQUITE
Papyrus

Choosing a Font for your Book

So, let's look at how to best go about choosing fonts from the vast array available to you. There are 4 key criteria you should consider when selecting a font, and I would recommend going through them in the order I have them listed here. Applying each criterion to your list will enable you to strike off those not suitable for your book until you are left with a short list of fonts that will work. It's then down to personal taste after that. The 4 key criteria are:

1. Readability
2. Suitability to Subject
3. Suitability to Audience
4. Aesthetics

1. Readability

It's a fact that some fonts are easier to read than others so it should come as no surprise that the typeface you choose for your book could influence its success on several levels. Imagine yourself flicking through a book you have picked off a shelf and having difficulty reading it. It's unlikely that you are going to buy it, right?

Now let's say you have purchased a book online (where you weren't able to flick through it first). As you are reading it, you start to get headaches from having to concentrate a bit harder because the font choice and formatting just aren't as polished as they should be. Chances are you are not going to finish the book, or if you do, you're not going to enjoy it as much and possibly leave it a bad review.

Both scenarios negatively influence the success of your book. By ignoring the readability of your font choices, you either risk not selling many books or getting poor reviews which in turn could negatively influence future sales.

VS

Top Tip:

Pay very close attention to how readable your chosen fonts are, and especially how they read in a large block of text. Most font management programs like Suitcase or Font Doctor allow you to preview a sample passage of text (such as a poem) in any chosen font. Google Fonts also offer the same feature, which is a great place to get some initial inspiration. I am not going to make any specific recommendations on which fonts to use at this stage but will return to this subject later in the article once we have reviewed the other criteria that you should consider before making your ultimate decision.

2. Suitability to subject

Surprising as it might seem, some fonts suit some topics more than others. Indeed, many fonts have been specifically designed to convey an impression independent of the words they are used to form. These perceptual differences give rise to the possibility that choosing the wrong font could lead to a mismatch in your reader's mind between the literal meaning of your words and the visual impression conveyed by your choice of font.

This concept can be a little hard to grasp so here are two examples that might help.

As its name suggests, the font Comic Sans was inspired by the kind of lettering often used in comic books. Its purpose was to give a casual, relaxed impression suitable for speech bubbles, which makes it inappropriate for a serious topic such as a book on will-writing or the memoirs of a war vet.

On the flip side of the coin, take a font such as Palatino, which was designed to mirror the letters formed by the broad nib pens used by calligraphers of the 18th century. It would look out of place if used to typeset a satirical comedy or futuristic sci-fi thriller.

Twenty years from now you will be more disappointed by the things that you didn't do than by the ones you did do. So throw off the bowlines. Sail away from the safe harbor. Catch the trade winds in your sails. Explore. Dream. Discover. - Mark Twain

vs

Twenty years from now you will be more disappointed by the things that you didn't do than by the ones you did do. So throw off the bowlines. Sail away from the safe harbor. Catch the trade winds in your sails. Explore. Dream. Discover. - Mark Twain

Top Tip:

Make sure that the font you choose for your book is appropriate to its subject matter. To help you do this, look at other books on similar topics and note which fonts they use. Some larger publishers make this easy by listing the font used in the front of the book on the page where they show the publishers' details. Alternatively, there are various online tools such as an app called WhatTheFont which makes it possible to identify a font from an image captured by your smartphone camera.

3. Suitability to the audience

Another factor to consider when choosing a font for your book is the nature of your target reader. To understand what I mean let's use a fashion analogy. If you were going out to the beach on the weekend with your friends, would you wear the same clothes as you would if meeting an important client in the head office of a blue-chip company? You'd dress to suit the circumstances, wouldn't you?

Well, the same principle holds true when you choose your font. Always make sure you choose a font that is appropriate for your primary readership. Take age for example. Sans-serif fonts are often preferred by younger readers because of their simpler shapes and modern feel, whereas an older audience will be drawn to a more traditional serif font.

By choosing a font that is inappropriate for your audience, you risk putting them off buying your book. For example, a successful entrepreneur may think your book is not serious enough, or a stressed-out university student who just wants a relaxing romance novel to take her mind off studying may think your book is too serious.

> Twenty years from now you will be more disappointed by the things that you didn't do than by the ones you did do. So throw off the bowlines. Sail away from the safe harbor. Catch the trade winds in your sails. Explore. Dream. Discover. - Mark Twain

vs

> Twenty years from now you will be more disappointed by the things that you didn't do than by the ones you did do. So throw off the bowlines. Sail away from the safe harbor. Catch the trade winds in your sails. Explore. Dream. Discover. - Mark Twain

Top Tip:

When choosing a font for your book, try and put yourself in your readers' shoes. Who are they, what are their lives like, what will appeal to them, and what do they hold important? These things can point you in the direction of a design style that will resonate with them. Once you have a persona of your reader in mind, go through your list of fonts and see which ones fit that image.

4. Aesthetics

As well as considering the basic readability of your font choices, I believe it's also important that you think about more subjective elements such as perception and beauty. These topics are collectively referred to as Aesthetics and depend very heavily on personal taste.

This criterion is all about gut feeling. Does the font feel right? Does it give your book the sense of quality that you are looking for? Is it beautifully balanced? Is it interesting?

If you have considered all the previous criteria carefully, there are no right or wrong choices when you get to this stage. The only word of warning that I would give you is to bear in mind whether your personal persona is representative of your target audience or not. If you're not, then your personal tastes should not play as important a role as those of your readers. But at the end of the day, it is YOUR book, and you must be happy with the results, or you are less likely to put your all into selling it.

Top Tip:

Think about whether you are your target audience or not. If you are, then chose a font that works for you. If you are not, then get the opinion of someone who IS your target audience. Which of the fonts in your shortlist do they like? Don't forget to ask 'why' they prefer one to the other. Even if they are not 100% sure of the answer, the insight will help you design better books in the future.

Recommendations:

So, now that you know a bit more about what to consider when choosing a font for your book, I want to share a few of my personal favourites with you as well as a few fonts to avoid. This list is by no means exhaustive but, if time is limited, you can choose a font from this list, safe in the knowledge that it will serve your purpose well.

Note: I have intentionally kept this list to fonts that are common on most modern computers as well as some available for free through Google Fonts.

Recommended fonts:		Fonts to avoid:	
Font	**Usage Comments**	**Font**	**Usage Comments**
Garamond (serif)	A professional looking serif font that is clean, legible, and well balanced. Garamond has a more classical feel that will suit a serious subject.	Courier (Serif)	This font was designed to look like the output from an old-fashioned typewriter is supposed to radiate dignity and prestige, but as it isn't proportional, it can make your book layout look messy.
Georgia (Serif)	A less commonly used alternative to Garamond.	Times New Roman (Serif)	This is an elegant, classy font but it is the default for many word processors. I think there are better, more distinctive alternatives.
Caslon Old Face (Serif)	This serif font is used for the main text in many books thanks to its excellent readability and comfortable and inviting feel. Just be aware that it has a very traditional look that can make large amounts of text look dated, but is perfect for any sort of period topics.	Bodoni (Serif)	Due to its high contrast between thick and thin strokes, Bodoni can be very hard to read in large amounts. If the Art Deco feel of this font suits your subject, consider only using it for headlines.

Recommended fonts:		Fonts to avoid:	
Font	Usage Comments	Font	Usage Comments
Merriweather (Serif)	Even in lighter weights, Merriweather has a solid, dependable feel to it that will lend text a feeling of authority. It is also very easy to read, so good for older readers or those with poor eyesight.	Slabo (Serif)	Slabo is what's known as a 'slab serif'. It has serif flourishes, but they tend to be very square and blunt. This bluntness can make for unattractive blocks of text and can give your book a sense of 'don't care' about it.
Helvetica (Sans-serif)	A more creative alternative to the Aerial which, as a sans-serif font, is appropriate for titles and subtitles.	Arial (Sans-serif)	This is a very common font, and many designers think that it has been overused. I personally feel it lacks character and can be boring.
Open Sans (Sans Serif)	This is a great sans-serif font that combines some of the traditional letter shapes from serif fonts (such as the bowl of the lowercase 'g') with the modern readability of a sans-serif.	Eurostile (Sans-serif)	This font has an odd mix of modern and traditional letter forms and so can be a bit confusing regarding suitability.

Recommended fonts:

Font	Usage Comments
Century Gothic (Sans-Serif)	A great alternative to Helvetica or Arial that tend to be overused. It has a very round and open feel to it that makes it very modern. Just be wary that it can be space hungry, so use with slight negative tracking.
Roboto (San-Serif)	This is a very clear and concise font that is easy to read in all weights and is ideal for both headings and body copy.

Fonts to avoid:

Font	Usage Comments
Impact (Sans-Serif)	This font, even in it's lightest weight, is very thick and heavy. It can come across as very "shouty" and will look very intimidating set in large amounts of text.
Gill Sans (Sans-Serif)	Gill Sans has a couple of letters within it's set that also contain serif flourishes (such as the lower case 'a'). In some fonts, this works, but with Gill Sans I find they stand out and can come across as a mistake.

Making your final decision

Ultimately, choosing the font for your book is a subjective decision. To help you do this, I would recommend that you draw up a shortlist of two to three fonts that you like and then have your designer typeset a few sample pages in each of your chosen fonts.

Even slight differences between individual fonts become much more noticeable when you see them as a large block of text.

And remember to print those samples out, as fonts can look, read, and feel very different on screen compared how they look when they are printed.

10 Best Fonts to Make Your Book Look Like a Bestseller

A lot of authors who opt to typeset their own books ask me "What are the Best Fonts to use for my book"? And they invariably expect me to just give them the name of a font that they can then go and use knowing that it will be right.

Unfortunately, there is a lot more to it than that. Several different factors go into choosing the right fonts for your book. Such as subject matter, target audience, the purpose of your book, and how you anticipate readers will use your book. Even down to what budget you have available for printing and the target cover price.

But I realise that for the average author who doesn't have a background in graphic design or an understanding of typography, considering those sorts of questions in relation to font choice is a bit overwhelming. So, I've written this article to give you a basic primer on the sorts of things you should consider when choosing your fonts. I'll even give you a list of my favourite free-to-use Google fonts to get you started.

Why Font Choice is Important

Before we get stuck into looking at any particular fonts, let's look at why this decision is so important in determining the potential success of your book.

Back in 2017, I wrote an article titled "The Science of How We Read, & How to Use it to Build a Better Book" in which I went into the mechanics of how the human eye views and processes written words and how to format your book to make that process easier for your reader.

In the article I touched on several points related to font choice: the style of font (i.e., serif, sans serif or display), font readability and how it relates to perceived task difficulty and font size.

Style of Font

There is much contention in the design world as to whether Serif or Sans Serif fonts are easier to read. However, the latest brain research suggests that, when it comes to readability, there is little solid evidence either way. So, the choice between serif or sans serif generally comes down to personal preference. If you are mindful of how that font is perceived in terms of purpose.

The big distinction comes in when discussing display fonts. The advent of computers and digital typesetting has opened the door to a plethora of modern decorative fonts which, although more stylish, are often harder to read. All the reading theories I discussed in the article depend to some degree on being able to decipher individual letter characteristics. If the font you choose is so decorative that the letter forms are not immediately clear, it will take the brain longer to decide what each letter is, causing the reader to get fatigued and possibly lose interest.

Font Readability & Perceived Task Difficulty

Research indicates that the harder a passage is to read, the more challenging the action written about will appear to be to the reader. By testing the reader's reactions to the same set of instructions presented in either an easy or a hard-to-read font, the researchers could show a direct correlation between readability and perceived task difficulty.

Font Size

Clearly, font size has an impact on readability. Why else do you think we have "small print" in most contracts? All other things being equal, the smaller the font size, the harder it is to read. But, on the other hand, the bigger the font, the more pages in your book, and the more expensive it will be to print. Research suggests that the minimum print size for readability is 9pt. However, it should be noted that the design characteristics of the font used can have an impact on this. More on that in a moment.

So as you can see, choosing the right fonts for your book is an important decision that can have a direct impact on how readers will interpret and perceive your book. If you want to read the full "Science of How We Read" article, you can find it here: https://swatt-books.co.uk/the-science-of-how-we-read-and-how-to-use-it-to-build-a-better-book

My List of the Best Fonts for Books

So now that you understand why font choice is important, let's look at the options you have available to you.

I'm going to focus mainly on font choice for the body copy as that is what 99% of your book will contain. I will add a few notes regarding how to best pair these fonts either with each other or with appropriate display fonts for headings and titles at the end of the article.

Serif

So, your first main option for a font is Serif; these are the fonts with the little bits added to individual letters. They are also the most common choice for book body copy as they are the first type of fonts used in commercial printing.

Because of that history, serif fonts will give your book a more traditional feel. I will normally default to a serif font for books with a more serious subject matter where the author wants to be perceived as an authority on the subject. I tend also to use serif fonts for books that are longer in length where there will be a high number of pages with solid text unbroken by headings and subheadings (such as fiction or long-tail textbooks).

Merriweather

https://fonts.google.com/specimen/Merriweather

Merriweather

Glyph

M
m

Characters

ABCČĆDĐEFGHIJKLMNOPQRSŠTU
VWXYZŽabcčćdđefghijklmnopqrs
štuvwxyzžАБВГЃДЂЕЁЄЖЗЅИІЇЙ
ЈКЛЉМНЊОПРСТЋУЎФХЦЧЏШЩ
ЪЫЬЭЮЯабвгѓдђеёєжзѕиіїйјкл
љмнњопрстћуўфхцчџшщъыьэ
юяĂÂÊÔƠƯăâêôơư1234567890'?'
"!"(%)[#]{@}/&\<-+÷×=>®©$€
£¥¢:;,.*

Merriweather is by far my favourite serif available from the Google Fonts platform. It was designed by font foundry Sorkin Type and comes with a good choice of font weights as well as italic options. It has a generous 'x-height', which means the text ends up being very legible without having to resort to a larger font size. The letters are also very slightly condensed which means that it is a very space-efficient font. Just note that the numerals of this font are in an old-style format, so some aspects of certain numbers will sit slightly below the baseline. Merriweather also has a sans-serif version which makes font pairing very easy for novice typesetters.

EB Garamond

https://fonts.google.com/specimen/EB+Garamond

EB Garamond

Glyph

Ee

Characters

ABCČĆDĐEFGHIJKLMNOPQRSŠTUV
WXYZŽabcčćdđefghijklmnopqrsštuvwx
yzžАБВГГДЂЕЁЄЖЗЅИІЇЙЈКЛЉМН
ЊОПРСТЋУЎФХЦЧЏШЩЪЫЬЭЮЯа
бвггдђеёєжзѕиіїйјклљмнњопрстћуўфхц
чџшщъыьэюяΑΒΓΔΕΖΗΘΙΚΛΜΝΞΟΠΡ
ΣΤΥΦΧΨΩαβγδεζηθικλμνξοπρστυφχψωά
Άέ'Εέ'ΗίϊΐΊόΌύΰϋ'Υ Ÿ ἀἁὲἐἠἡὶἱὸὑὺὐὼώΏ Ã
ÂÊÔÕUãâêôõu1234567890'?'"!"(%)[#]{
@}/&\<-+÷×=>®©$€£¥¢:;,.*

EB Garamond is intended to be a modern revival of Claude Garamont's famous 16th-century humanist typeface 'Garamond' designed by Georg Duffner and Octavio Pardo. Due to its classical roots, EB Garamond is a very traditional style font and is great for authors looking to add a classical feel to their books. It contains an extensive character set including Greek so is ideal for scientific or mathematical subjects. There is a wide range of weights and italics available in the set but be mindful that this font has been designed to give italics the impression of being slightly larger than non-italic text.

Lora

https://fonts.google.com/specimen/Lora

Lora

Glyph	Characters
Ll	ABCČĆDĐEFGHIJKLMNOPQRSŠTU VWXYZŽabcčćdđefghijklmnopqrsšt uvwxyzžАБВГЃДЂЕЁЄЖЗѕИІЇЙЈКЛ ЉМНЊОПРСТЋУЎФХЦЏЧЏШЩЪЫЬ ЭЮЯабвгѓдђеёєжзѕиіїйјклљмнњо прстћуўфхцџчџшщъыьэюяĂÂÊÔÖÙ ăâêôöủ1234567890'?'"!"(%)[#]{@}/ &\<-+:×=>®©$€£¥¢:;,.*

Lora is a well-balanced contemporary serif with roots in calligraphy designed by font foundry Cyreal. It is a text typeface with moderate contrast that is well-suited for large amounts of body text. Its calligraphic background gives the little finials (the bits that make up the serifs) a much softer feel than some of the more traditional serif fonts. This makes it ideal for more personal or artistic subjects. Just note that it is only available in 4 styles.

Playfair Display

https://fonts.google.com/specimen/Playfair+Display

Playfair Display

Glyph

Pp

Characters

ABCČĆDDEFGHIJKLMNOPQRSŠTUV
WXYZŽabcčćddefghijklmnopqrsštuv
wxyzžАБВГДЕЁЖЗИЙКЛМНОПРСТ
УФХЦЧШЩЪЫЬЭЮЯабвгдеёжзийк
лмнопрстуфхцчшщъыьэюяÄÂÊÔÓ
ÜãâêôõűÍ1234567890'?'"!"(%)|#|{a}/&
\<-+÷×=>®©$¢£¥¢::..*

Playfair is a very high-contrast font which means that there is a large difference between the thick and thin parts of each letter. Generally, this would mean that it wouldn't be suitable for small text sizes, however, this font also features a generous 'x' height similar to Merriweather, so that text set in Playfair is still easily legible at common body copy sizes. It was designed by Claus Eggers Sørensen as a modern twist on fonts popular during the Art Deco period of the late 18th century such as "Baskerville". It features a good number of various styles and weights and when you download the full font set also comes with a dedicated small caps version as well as a set of discretionary ligatures (where certain common letter pairs such as 'th' and 'st' are joined together) which can give the text a very distinctive character.

Crimson Text

https://fonts.google.com/specimen/Crimson+Text

Crimson Text

Glyph

Cc

Characters

A B C D E F G H I J K L M N O P Q R S T U V W X Y Z
a b c d e f g h i j k l m n o p q r s t u v w x y z 1 2 3 4 5 6 7 8 9
0 ' ? ' " ! " (%) [#] { @ } / & \ < - + ÷ × = > ® © $ € £ ¥ ¢ : ; , . *

The final serif in my list of favourites is Crimson Text, which is a beautifully elegant old-style font designed by Sebastian Kosch specifically for book production. It is very easy to read and as a font set comes with a number of little niceties such as old-style numerals, small caps and mathematical symbols. There are a total of 6 styles and weights available, and it makes for a great text 'workhorse'.

San Serif

Your second main option of font is Sans Serif, and unsurprisingly these are the fonts without the little bits added to individual letters. They are a byproduct of the digital age and were developed because original computer screens just didn't have the pixel density to render minute detail.

Because of their origins, sans serif fonts will give your book a more modern and contemporary feel. I will normally revert to a sans serif font for books with a more contemporary subject matter or books where the author wants a modern look.

Monsterrat

https://fonts.google.com/specimen/Montserrat

Montserrat

Glyph

Characters

ABCČĆDĐEFGHIJKLMNOPQRSŠT
UVWXYZŽabcčćdđefghijklmnop
qrsštuvwxyzžАБВГЃДЂЕЁЄЖЗЅИ
ІЇЙЈКЛЉМНЊОПРСТЋУЎФХЦЧЏ
ШЩЪЫЬЭЮЯабвгѓдђеёєжзѕиіїй
јклљмнњопрстћуўфхцчџшщъыь
эюяĂÂÊÔƠƯăâêôơư1234567890'
?'"!"(%)[#]{@}/&\<-+÷×=>®©$€£¥
¢:;,.*

Monsterrat is one of the more elegant sans serif fonts in my opinion and was inspired by turn-of-the-century urban typography posters in Buenos Aires. Monsterrat comes in a large number of weights and styles and lends itself to a wide variety of uses from main headers to body copy and small print. The font has a full set of Cyrillic and Greek characters and also has a set of Alternates and dedicated underlined sister fonts which make it extremely versatile.

Raleway

https://fonts.google.com/specimen/Raleway

Raleway is an elegant sans serif font original intended for headings and other large text size uses. Initially designed by Matt McInerney as a single thin weight, it was expanded into a 9-weight family by Pablo Impallari and Rodrigo Fuenzalida in 2012. Because of its large 'x-height', it can also be used for body copy as long as you set it with generous line spacing.

Roboto

https://fonts.google.com/specimen/Roboto

Roboto

Glyph | Characters

ABCČĆDĐEFGHIJKLMNOPQRSŠTUV
WXYZŽabcčćdđefghijklmnopqrsštuv
wxyzžАБВГЃДЂЕЁЄЖЗЅИЇЙЈКЛЉ
МНЊОПРСТЋУЎФХЦЧЏШЩЪЫЬЭЮ
Яабвгѓдђеёєжзѕиїйјклљмнњопрст
ћуўфхцчџшщъыьэюяΑΒΓΔΕΖΗΘΙΚΛ
ΜΝΞΟΠΡΣΤΥΦΧΨΩαβγδεζηθικλμνξο
πρστυφχψωáÁéÉèÉ̀ΗιÌïÏíÍóÓùÙüÜÝÝ̀ΩΆÃÂ
ÊÔÔŬăâêôơư1234567890'?'"!"(%)[#]
{@}/&\<-+÷×=>®©$€£¥¢:;,.*

Roboto is a great sans-serif font for portraying strength and masculinity. It has a very geometric structure; however, the overall proportions of each letter have not been forced into a set width which makes for a more comfortable reading experience. It was designed by Christian Robertson and features a large number of weights and styles as well as Condensed and Slab sister fonts that make font pairing very easy.

Oswald

https://fonts.google.com/specimen/Oswald

Oswald

Glyph

Oo

Characters

ABCČĆDĐEFGHIJKLMNOPQRSŠTUVWXYZŽab cčćdđefghijklmnopqrsštuvwxyzžАБВГЃДЂE ЁЄЖЗЅИІЇЙЈКЛЉМНЊОПРСТЋУЎФХЦЧЏШ ЩЪЫЬЭЮЯабвггдђеёєжзѕиіїйјклљмнњопр стћуўфхцчџшщъыьэюяĂÂÊÔÔUăâêôơu123 4567890'?'"!"(%)[#]{@}/&\<-+÷×=>®©$ €£¥¢:;,.*

Oswald was initially designed to better fit the pixel grid of standard digital screens, hence its slightly condensed appearance. This condensed structure makes it ideal for main titles and headings, however as it does not contain any italic styles so it's not suitable for large amounts of body copy. Despite missing any italic options, Oswald does come in 6 different weights making it very flexible for books with extensive heading hierarchies.

Open Sans

https://fonts.google.com/specimen/Open+Sans

Open Sans

Glyph | Characters

ABCČĆDĐEFGHIJKLMNOPQRSŠTUV
WXYZŽabcčćdđefghijklmnopqrsštu
vwxyzžАБВГЃДЋЕЁЄЖЗЅИІЇЙЈКЛЉ
МНЊОПРСТЋУЎФХЦЧЏШЩЪЫЬЭЮ
Яабвгѓдђеёєжзѕиіїйјклљмнњопрс
тћуўфхцчџшщъыьэюяΑΒΓΔΕΖΗΘΙΚ
ΛΜΝΞΟΠΡΣΤΥΦΧΨΩαβγδεζηθικλμν
ξοπρστυφχψωάΆέΈέΉἱϊἷΊόΌύΰῦΎΫ
ΏΆÂÊÔÖÚăâêôơư1234567890'?'"!"(
%)[#]{@}/&\<-+÷×=>®©$€£¥¢:;,.*

My final sans serif font of choice is Open Sans which is what's known as a 'humanist' font (which basically means that they are more organic and have a more handmade feel without being decorative like scripts). It was designed by Steve Matterson and boosts an extensive 897-character set including all standard Latin, Greek and Cyrillic letters as well as a wide range of symbols and glyphs which makes it ideal for foreign language translations and math/science-based subjects. Unlike many sans serif fonts, it has been optimised for print as well as web and mobile and has excellent legibility.

Conclusion

So, there you have it; my list of the top 10 best fonts for books. I want to leave you with a quick insight into how to pair your fonts – which is the process of matching different fonts within the same design. I will most likely go into more depth on this subject in a future article, but here are a few basic tips to get you started.

1. Pairing a Serif with a Sans Serif is always a great trick for adding variety to your book and making headings really stand out without having to resort to large font sizes.
2. Look for fonts that have a wide variety of weights and styles so that you have plenty of options to play with contrast between headings and body copy.
3. Consider fonts that have sister fonts within the same family (such as Monsterrat and Monsterrat Sans, or Roboto and Roboto Slab) as they have been designed specifically to work together.
4. When in doubt, see what other people have paired their fonts with. Google Fonts has a great feature of providing suggest font pairing for the majority of their fonts, though they tend to be limited to their most popular options. If you want a bit of variety, check out the website FontPair (https://fontpair.co) which has a huge list of suggested font pairings of Google Fonts and is a great site I use when needing a bit of extra inspiration.

5 Word Manuscript Tips to Save Time when Typesetting Your Book

Let's face it, writing and publishing a book can be time-consuming. But there are a few ways that you can save yourself a little bit of time that can make your book more professional in the end. Here are my top 5 tips to employ when writing your manuscript in Word that can save both you and your typesetter time on your next book.

1. Use stylesheets

This is the biggest time-saving tip of them all! If you're not familiar with what stylesheets are, they are a collection of grouped formatting decisions. So instead of having to manually set the font, size, colour, spacing, etc. to make a line of text a heading, you simply select a Heading stylesheet. Microsoft Word comes bundled with dozens of pre-set stylesheets for every type of content type you might need in a book from titles and headings, to captions, quotes, lists, endnotes, references, and table of contents entries.

To access stylesheets, simply turn on the "Styles Pane" in the Home tab of any open Word document. From there, you have the option of clearing any existing formatting and then applying any style to a highlighted section of text. Remember, consistency is king – it doesn't matter which formatting styles you use as long as you use them consistently throughout the entire book.

How Does it Save You Time?

Using stylesheets saves you from manually having to format each content type of your book. So, if you think of your average non-fiction book of 50k words; you may have 10 chapters. Each chapter may have 4-5 main headings, and each of those headings may have 2-3 subheadings. You may have a couple of quotes per chapter as well as some references. Then let's not forget any emphasis formatting such as bolds, underlines or italics. When you start adding up all of the formatting that goes into a book, being able to apply all of that formatting with just a single click as opposed to manually every time; the timesaving starts to add up.

Stylesheets also have the added benefit of maintaining consistency throughout your book. It can sometimes be difficult to remember how you formatted the main title in Chapter 1 by the time you get to Chapter 9. Using stylesheets means that you don't need to remember; Word remembers it for you.

Using stylesheets can also save your designer/typesetter even more time than it saves you. If you are 100% consistent in applying stylesheets when writing your manuscript, your design can then use your stylesheets as a roadmap for applying the final design to your typeset book. If they are skilled enough, they can even use your stylesheets to automatically apply the correct formatting to your book, reducing the typesetting time by more than half – which could have the knock-on effect of reducing the cost they charge you.

2. Use the headers and footers

Using the Headers and Footers feature in Word isn't so much of a timesaving tip as a general consistency and sanity-saving tip. It's fairly obvious to most authors to use the Headers and Footers in Word for the 'page furniture' of your book (the title and author name at the top and page numbers at the bottom – or vice versa if you choose). However, I have seen the odd manuscript in my time where these have been manually added to each page… Just don't do it! The feature is there; use it.

To access the Headers and Footers feature in Word, simply double-click the top or bottom of a page outside of the text margin. The main body of text will grey out slightly, and you will be able to type directly inside the header and footer (which will be conveniently marked for you in the left-hand margin). To go back to editing the content, simply double-click anywhere in the main text body.

How Does it Save You Time?

Using the headers and footers to format your page furniture is one of those "set & forget" things. You only need to do it once when you start your manuscript, and then you never have to bother with it again. If you're an advanced Word user, you can go so far as to customise these for each chapter, but it's not necessary.

If you are publishing with a very limited budget and are planning on doing your own design and typesetting using Word, using the headers and footers for your page furniture will also ensure laser-accurate consistency throughout the book. There's nothing worse than flipping through a book and seeing the page numbers dance around – even slightly.

If you are contracting a designer to typeset your book and you Haven't used Headers and Footers, then your design will need to manually remove each instance of your page furniture. This added formatting time could cause your designer to charge you extra.

3. Single space after sentences

This particular point often causes quite a bit of controversy. The convention of using two spaces after a full stop is a throwback to the age of the typewriter where universal letter spacing meant that a single space between a full stop and the next sentence often wasn't wide enough, so typists learned to type a double space. But with the advent of computer word processing, digital printing and variable-width fonts, the necessity for the extra space is no longer required, it became personal taste – and background. If you had any formal design training after the 1980s, it was drilled into you that the font designers had ensured that the space after a full stop was the perfect amount, and a double space would look wrong. As such, the publishing industry has adopted the single-space rule.

How Does it Save You Time?
The amount of time it will save you during the typing of your manuscript is going to be very minimal, however, the time it will save your designer/typesetter in not having to remove all the extra spaces will make a difference.

Again, if you are looking to do your own typesetting it will ensure that your book looks professional and not just bodged together in Word.

4. Use 'space after' between paragraphs

Using the Space After feature in between paragraphs as opposed to an extra carriage return is another one of those tips that won't have much impact on your overall writing time but will have a huge impact on your designers' time.

Using an extra carriage return has the potential of causing problems if they happen to fall exactly on a page break. You could end up with one of these extra returns sitting at the very top of a new page, meaning that your first line of text on that page doesn't sit in line with the first line of text on the opposite page.

You may be thinking "No big deal, I'll just delete that extra return – problem solved". What happens if during the review and proofreading process, some of the text previous to that section changes and the new paragraph suddenly ends up at the bottom of the previous page, or the text gets shifted up to the new page? You suddenly find yourself with two paragraphs that don't have any space between them...

Using Space After eliminates the need for extra carriage returns at all and ensures that no matter where your page breaks fall, you will always have the right amount of space between paragraphs.

To access 'space after' simply click the Line and Paragraph Spacing icon in the Home tool ribbon and select Line Spacing Options…

How Does it Save You Time?

Using Space After is a function that can be built into your stylesheets, meaning one-click formatting for you. Many of the stylesheets that come bundled with Word already have some space before or after incorporated in them (specifically stylesheets dealing with headings and quotes).

But the main timesaving comes for your designer/typesetter as they do not have to manually remove all of those extra carriage returns. So once again, it is a tip that could potentially save you money as well as time.

5. Use page breaks between chapters

The benefits of utilizing page breaks instead of multiple carriage returns in between chapters are very similar to those of using 'space after'. Chapters in a book should always start on a fresh page – whether they start on a right-hand page or not is down to the preference of the author, but they need to be separate from the content of the previous chapter.

Some authors do this by adding in as many carriage returns as necessary to move the new chapter title onto the next page. However, any change to the text in the previous chapter can potentially have the effect of moving where that new chapter starts.

To insert a page break at the end of each chapter, simply select the Pages icon from the Insert tool ribbon and select Page Break.

How Does it Save You Time?

Using page breaks instead of multiple returns can save you time in manually hitting return until your new chapter title finally clicks over to the next page. But primarily it will save you the hassle of having to manually adjust the number of returns you need whilst editing. By using page breaks, your chapters are guaranteed to always start on a fresh page, no matter what changes you make to the text preceding it.

As for your designer/typesetter, it saves them the time of having to remove all those extra returns when it comes to setting your final content. Also, if they are clever in the way they import your Word document into InDesign or LaTex (whichever program they use), those page breaks will remain in place meaning they don't have to add them back in.

Conclusion

So, as you can see there are multiple ways that you can save little pockets of time whilst writing your book in Word that can then have even larger timesaving benefits when it comes to typesetting your final book artwork. All these little pockets of time can add up throughout a publishing project that could reduce your on-sale time by days, even weeks.

Plus, if you are planning on using Word to typeset your books' interior artwork, then these tips will also help you to produce a book that looks as professional as it can be without the aid of a trained designer/typesetter.

4 Great Book Design Resources if you're on a Budget

If you've been reading my blog for a while, you'll know the importance I place on good book design as a contributing factor to self-publishing success. But I do appreciate that there are a lot of first-time authors out there who simply do not have the budget available to pay for professional book design support when they are just starting out.

With that in mind, I want to share with you some no-cost/low-cost book design resources that can help you publish a good-quality book if you're on a tight budget.

#1. Canva + KDP File Setup Calculator (Free)

This first book design resource will help you with DIY book cover design.

We've all heard of how great Canva (https://www.canva.com) is for designing social media graphics, but did you know that you can also use it to create print graphics as well? Well, you can, but you'll need to know the exact dimensions of your book cover before you start.

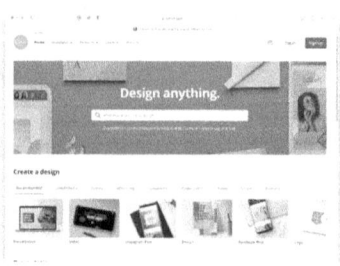

If you're publishing an eBook only, then it's simple – just design your cover to 1600px x 2400px and you only need to worry about what the front looks like. With a print book, however, you need to provide the front, back and spine as a single flat piece of artwork known as a book jacket. Enter Amazon's helpful (but difficult to locate) File Setup Calculator (https://kdp.amazon.com/en_US/help/topic/G200735480#setup_calculator). With this useful tool, simply enter your books' trim size, print type and page count into the Main Menu page, then click the Cover button. The calculator will then give you the exact dimensions your cover artwork needs to be and gives you guidelines on safe margins to use and placement on your ISBN barcode (which you can get from your ISBN agency when you purchase them).

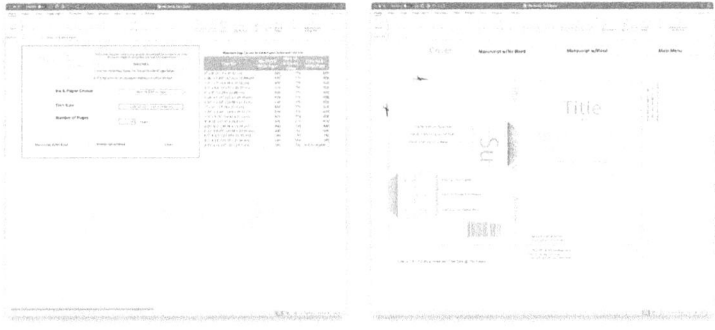

Once you have those measurements, go into Canva and select Custom Size. Change the measurement units to either mm, cm, or inches (whichever you prefer) and then enter the overall artwork width and height from the KDP File Setup Calculator and away you go.

IMPORTANT NOTE: When you go to download your completed artwork, be sure to select PDF Print from the download dropdown menu. If you don't, your artwork will not be high enough resolution for printing.

#2. FontPair.co + Google Fonts (Free)

This next pair of book design resources will help you with selecting the best fonts to use in your book.

I have written about how important font selection is in book design in the blog post "Why Font Choice is So Important in Book Design", but with so many fonts available to choose from it can be difficult to narrow it down. Introducing FontPair (https://fontpair.co). Font Pair is a typography site dedicated to helping creators use beautiful typography for their creative projects. Simply put, it shows you a selection of fonts that work well together that are available for free download from Google Fonts.

By being able to see how fonts interact with each other, it becomes much easier for you to choose fonts that are both suitable for book typesetting AND give the look and feel that relates to your genre/target audience. This is a resource that I use daily when selecting fonts to use in my clients' books.

Google Fonts (https://fonts.google.com) is a great font resource all on its own. It contains a library of over 3k different fonts suitable for nearly every design situation you can think of. Nearly all of the fonts in their library are licenced under either the Open Font Licence or Apache Licence, which allows you to use them freely in design projects and on products – print or digital, commercial or otherwise. Just be sure to double-check the Licence tab inside the individual fonts that you want to use before downloading.

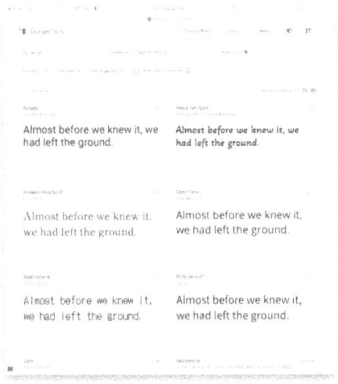

#3. KDP Manuscript Templates (Free)

The last free book design resource I have for you is another hidden gem available from Amazon KDP, and that's their manuscript templates (https://kdp.amazon.com/en_US/help/topic/G201834230). These are free Microsoft templates that Amazon have put together to help you format your manuscript consistently and to KDP specifications.

You have the option of downloading a completely blank template, or if you need a bit of direction, they have templates with sample content pre-loaded including formatted front matter (e.g., title page, table of contents) and chapters with placeholder text. This gives you the ability to customise the parts you want to keep and delete the sections you don't.

The download page for these templates also includes a very handy step-by-step guide on how to customise the templates to your needs, as well as links to more in-depth book-building guides for both Mac and PC versions of Microsoft Word, as well as Pages for Mac.

NOTE: It's worth spending a bit of time trawling through the Help Topics in Amazon KDP. You don't need to have signed up for an account to get access to them, but it can be very time-consuming to find what you are looking for as many of the sections can end up being 4 or 5 levels deep.

#4. 99 Designs (£239-£949)

All of the book design resources that we have looked at so far have been free-to-use options to help you DIY your book design. What if you don't have the time/skill/inclination to do it yourself, but also don't have the budget to work one-to-one with a professional graphic designer? Let me introduce you to 99 Designs.

99 Designs (https://99designs.co.uk) is a graphic design platform owned by Vistaprint. Like many freelance sourcing platforms, it allows you to connect with graphic designers from around the world. But unlike those other platforms, 99D also gives you the ability to publish a design contest in which their entire creative community can then submit ideas for your book cover, interior formatting, or any other design resource you may need for your book and then you pick your favourite.

I was introduced to this platform about 5 years ago by a client and I haven't looked back since. I use this platform to outsource all my client cover design, as well as using it for the design of both of my own book covers... which is high praise indeed.

Each contest has a tiered cost depending on how much prize money you want to offer the winning designer, but you can start a contest for as low as £239.

So, there you have it; my top 4 book design resources to help you publish a great book on a budget. If there are any other no-cost/low-cost resources that you have used that you want to share with the community, please do tell me about them in the comments.

5 Keys to a Killer Book Cover

I had a client last week that was really struggling with her book cover. We were coming up with some great ideas, but the more feedback she got from friends, colleagues, and target readers, the more confused she ended up being. It got me thinking about what ingredients are needed for a really great book cover. After much thought and looking through the multitude of covers on my own bookshelves, I realised that though there are many components that go into making a book cover; there are 5 key ingredients that separate the mighty from the mediocre. They are:

1. Title
2. Typography
3. Image
4. Relevance
5. Wow Factor

I realise that not every one of these keys is going to be applicable to every book. For example, you may want a text-only cover in which case you don't need to worry about getting your image spot on. Or you may want the image to be of you, which means you don't have to worry so much about relevance aside from the fact that it's your picture on the cover because you wrote it! Obviously, the more key ingredients you nail in your book cover, the more impact it is going to have. I think the table analogy is a great demonstrator of this concept… Imagine your book is sitting on a table in a bookstore, and the key ingredients are the legs of that table. If you only have one or two legs on your table, it's not even going to stand let alone stand up to the other books in the store. If you have three strong legs, your standing, but not very stable. The slightest knock is going to tip you over. Four legs and you have a good strong table, but make a table with five strong legs and nothing is knocking it over short of someone picking it up and launching it across the room!

The Job of a Book Cover

Before we get into what the 5 keys are all about, let's look at what the job of your book cover actually is. Centuries ago when mass-produced books were first being made, a book cover's job was simply to hold the book together and to provide a surface to stamp the title. But in today's day and age of advanced printing techniques, e-readers, and books being used as a viable business tool for millions of "authopreneurs", the job of the humble book cover has radically changed. A cover's purpose is still very simple, but also vastly more important now then ever before. **Its job is to make a reader want to pick your book up off the shelf!** There are many people who would argue with that statement by saying that a cover's job is to make a person want to buy your book, but I disagree. What your book is about is what will make a reader decide whether your book is right for them and ultimately whether they will buy it or not. The cover is what is going to draw that person to pick your book out of the dozens or hundreds of other books on the same subject to find out more about it. The cover is the honey, the lure, and the thing that catches the readers' attention and interest and makes them want to pick it up.

So now that you know what the purpose of your book cover is, let's explore how the 5 key ingredients work together to fulfil that purpose.

1. Title

Your book's title is the cornerstone of your cover; it's what sets the tone for everything to follow. Many great authors and book mentors will encourage you to come up with a title very early on in the writing process as it helps to give your writing direction. But remember that it isn't set in stone until it ends up on your front cover, so don't be afraid to let it evolve as your book does.

Ideally, your title should be catchy, easy to remember, and rolls off the tongue. If it doesn't, consider splitting it into a snappy title and explaining subtitle. Relevance to what your book is about is sometimes not always important. Let me explain. There is an NLP book called "Don't Think About Purple Spotted Oranges", which has to be one of the most random books titles I have ever come across. The supporting subtitle of "The manual you were meant to get with your brain" certainly steers you in the direction of what the book is about, but not quite a full reflection of a guide that helps you to improve your confidence and communication skills. However, its randomness was enough to make me pick it up to see what it was all about.

2. Typography

Because as a general rule, a front cover doesn't contain very much text, the text that is there must be exquisitely typeset. This is where a professional designer/typographer will be in their element! Lovingly kerning every letter of your title and making sure the tracking and kerning of every line is just so. Agonising over every little nuance of which font to choose and then perfecting the size and weight that font is set in… For those of you who are not typography weirdo's like me, your probably thinking "OMG what a faff! What can possibly be the point of all of that?" The point is that the benefits of really good typography are subliminal; only those trained in the art of typography can see the difference that it makes, but everyone picks up on it anyway. They don't necessarily know why some text is easier to read than others, or why a particular layout appeals to them more than another, but the typography plays a huge part in dictating that. So ignore it at your peril.

3. Image

The inclusion of imagery on a cover can be open to interpretation as to whether or not it is a necessary ingredient to a killer book cover. I did debate whether to include it in this list at all. But even though there are many great book covers out there that are text-only, I cannot ignore the impact that adding even a small graphic can have on the success of your book cover.

If you are going to include an image of some kind to your cover – whether it be a photograph, illustration, drawing, or just a simple icon or logo – it must be of the utmost quality. A photo that is blurry, poorly lit or too low a resolution, or an illustration that is badly drawn, bit-mapped, or incorrectly scanned will do your cover more harm than good. You also want to make sure that the image you choose matches the 'tone' of your book. The relevance of your image to your book is of a bit more importance than it was for your title. Don't just add an image to your cover because you think you "should"; it needs to have a reason for being there. Does it set the tone for the story, does it clarify what your book is about, or does it elicit an emotional connection with the reader? Once you know what purpose your image is going to serve on your cover, then it will be easier to select one that works with your book and not against it.

4. Relevance

We've talked a bit already about how certain elements of your cover need to have some relevance to the book inside, but relevance in terms of a key ingredient to a killer book cover is more about how everything relates to each other. Relevancy is how all the various elements come together in harmony to form a single unified cover that makes someone want to learn more. It's how your title relates to the story, how the fonts and typography relate to the title, how the style of imagery relates to the typography, and how your cover as a whole relates to the book and to the reader. There is no rulebook for this; there isn't a definitive list of do's and don'ts when it comes to how each element should relate to each other. But when it's right, you'll know it. Everything will just fit together perfectly, even if technically it shouldn't. Your readers will pick up on it too. The book will just FEEL right, and that's where the magic of a killer book cover really starts to kick in!

5. Wow Factor

The magic of a book cover that just feels right is amplified a million times when you add in the WOW! Just like with the term the 'X factor' in the entertainment industry; there isn't a list of criteria or a tried and tested formula for adding the wow factor to your book cover. It is something that your cover either has or it hasn't. Getting it takes a lot of experimentation, and pushing of boundaries to see what works and what doesn't. The tiniest change could be all it takes to go from woeful to wow. If you haven't found it yet, keep searching, because there are always second editions!

So there you have it, my list of 5 keys that you need for a killer book cover. To reward you for reading to the end I'm going to give you a secret tip… To apply all of these keys to your book cover effectively, you need to know who your book is for. Knowing your target audience is the hidden 6th key to nailing your book cover. I don't just mean narrowing down a demographic; I mean laser targeting who your one perfect reader is. Customer avatars that sales and marketing teams use are great tools to help you flesh out this ideal reader into a real person whom you can not only design your book cover for, but to write for as well.

How to Write a Kick-Ass Book Cover Design Brief

Aside from writing a good quality book, having a professional eye-catching book cover is of paramount importance to publishing a successful book. But if you're not very artistic or creative, how can you get a cover that does its' job of selling your hard work for you? You hire a professional to design it for you!

The problem is that many first-time authors have never had the experience of dealing with professional designers before. They don't know how to best convey the ideas in their head to someone else in such a way as to allow them to see what they see. Enter the Book Cover Design Brief. Every designer worth their salt will insist on having one, and even the majority of the only crowdsourcing platforms like 99Designs and Fiver make it part of their job listing process.

This article is going to look at what goes into writing a great book cover design brief that will ensure you and your designer are on the same page, and that they have the information they need to design a kick-ass book cover that will make your book shine.

What is a Book Cover Design Brief?

First things first, just in case you've not heard the term 'design brief' before, it is a document that details everything a designer needs to know about your book for them to design a suitable cover for it. It touches on things like specifications, text, images and ideas, but also gives them an insight into what the book is all about and who your target reader is.

Anyone with a copy of Photoshop can design a pretty-looking book cover, but if it doesn't relate to the content inside or doesn't capture the attention of the specific audience it is intended for, then it's nothing more than a pretty picture. That's the purpose of a Book Cover Design Brief; to give the designer the information needed to make that pretty picture *relevant*.

What Should a Book Cover Design Brief Include?

Four main areas make up a good book cover design brief:

- Specifications
- Content
- Background
- Creative Direction

Let's go into more detail on how to approach each section.

Specifications

This section covers the basic technical and physical specifications of your book. It should include things like:

- Trim size
- Binding type (paperback, casebound hardback, or jacketed hardback)
- Spine width (you will probably have to estimate this to start with, but can finalise it once you have a definitive page count)
- Cover finish (gloss or matte)

You also want to give the designer an indication of how the cover is going to be produced. Are you going to be taking it to a traditional printer to produce a print run of hundreds of copies, or will you be publishing using a Print on Demand model? If you're going to go down the print-on-demand route, your designer will need to know which platform(s) you will be using to ensure that the files they produce are technically compliant.

Content

This section provides all the details of the actual content that needs to be included on the cover. Don't forget that this needs to consider the back cover and spine as well as the front cover. It should include:

- Main title
- Subtitle (if applicable)
- How you want your author name to appear (including any designations that need to appear after your name)
- Back cover blurb
- Short author bio for the back cover (not required, but is a good idea to include if you have space)
- ISBN barcode (if you don't have one yet, be sure the designer knows to allocate space for it)
- Publisher name and icon (again not mandatory, but gives your book a more professional look)
- Any additional text that you want to include (for example a one-line review, or accolade)

You should also give some thought to any images that you definitely want to be included on your book cover. This typically includes an author headshot if you're having one and if some particular graphics or logos need to be included. Be sure that you have permission to use any images and that you are sending your designer the highest possible resolution of those images. A good rule of thumb for photographs is the larger the file size the higher the resolution.

Background

This section is less about how your book cover is going to look and more about the *intention* and *purpose* of your book. It should include:

- A bit of background on what your book is about
- What the purpose of your book is and what do you expect readers to do/feel/learn once they've read it
- A brief description of who your target audience is (I have a blog article that talks all about how to determine your ideal reader that you can read here if you need help)

When describing your ideal reader, be sure to include both *who* they are and *what* they are. Think about things like general and socio-economic demographics, but also interests, pain points and common traits. All of this will help your designer to get into the head of your target audience and make design decisions that will appeal directly to them.

Creative Direction

This final section is where you give your designer a bit of initial direction and guidance. There are no hard and fast rules about what you need to include here, but I suggest thinking about:

- What you like and don't like
- If there are any branding guidelines in terms of fonts or colours that need or you want to be incorporated
- If you have a particular idea for what you want your cover to look like, try to describe it as best as possible (even consider drawing out a rough sketch)
- Give examples of other book covers that you like the look of
- Think about what types of design styles would be appropriate for your cover (i.e. minimalist, fun, bold, luxurious)

If you don't have any particular images that you need your designer to incorporate, but want to explore the idea of using imagery, let them know whether you are open to the idea of using stock images or not. If so, give them an indication as to how much budget you have for the purchase of stock images. Also, give them an indication as to whether you prefer those images to be photographic or illustrative.

Likewise, if you don't want to use any imagery on your cover, be specific in telling your designer to work with text only.

Benefits of a Good Book Cover Design Brief

The benefits that you get from writing a good book cover design brief far outweigh the time and thought process it takes to get it right. Providing your designer with a clear, concise, and details book cover design brief means that you will be far more likely to get a book cover that you not only will love but will make your job of marketing and selling your book that much easier.

Though it flies in the face of the age-old saying "don't judge a book by its cover"; that is precisely what readers will be doing with your book if they have not heard of you before. So it is well worth the time and investment to get it right.

One final thought that I want to leave you with…

On the odd occasion, I have heard authors say that this process of writing a book cover design brief sounds counterproductive. I even heard one author go so far as to say, 'If I have to explain everything that I want and don't want, I might as well do it myself'. There are two main reasons why that is just not the case.

A) As talented as professional graphic designers are, they are not telepathic. They cannot see the image that you have in your head. If you want to have any hope of getting what you want out of the process of working with a designer, you need to communicate what you want and don't want.

B) No self-respecting graphic designer is just going to blindly copy what you tell them you want to see. They will draw on their training and understanding of design theory, layout, colour psychology and typography to take your ideas and refine them into a professional piece of design that is fit for purpose.

I hope you have found that insight useful for when it comes time for you to write your first (or next) book cover design brief. If you want some more advice on effective book cover design, check out my blog article "5 Keys to a Killer Book Cover", or you can arrange a 1 to 1 consultation with me to discuss your book and its cover by clicking over to my Online Diary and booking a Digital Coffee.

Part 3: ...on Publishing

50 Shades of Self-Publishing

Since self-publishing has grown in popularity and accessibility, the opinion of the literary world as to whether it is a good thing or a bad thing has been varied and polarising. People either love it or loathe it, they tout it as either the destruction of the publishing industry or the route to writers' utopia! I exaggerate of course, but you get the drift.

In this article, I want to explore some of the opinions that have appeared in the media about self-publishing and weigh in with my take on the matter.

The destruction of the publishing industry

Change in any industry can be a scary thing for most people to accept, which inevitably leads to resistance and backlash; and the shift towards self-publishing is no exception.

Take Ros Barber for example. An author with a long career in traditional publishing, who in 2016 wrote an article for the Guardian newspaper[15] in which she said,

> *"You risk looking like an amateur… Good writers need even better editors. They need brilliant cover designers. They need imaginative marketers and well-connected publicists. All these things are provided by a traditional publisher, and what's more, it doesn't cost you a penny. They pay you! If a self-published author wants to avoid looking like an amateur, they'd better be prepared to shell out some serious cash to get professional help in all the areas where they don't excel. And I mean serious."*

Then you have renowned book critic Ron Charles, who submitted an open letter to the Washington Post[16] titled "No, I Don't Want to Read your Self-Published Book" in which he cited concerns that there were too many self-published authors and that self-published books lacked quality, and where published by authors with little understanding of their audience or the market.

Or this quote from professional blogger Tom Jager in an article for Independent Publishing Magazine[17]:

> *"The market is suffocated with worthless literature, and self-publishing contributes towards that mess."*

Not to mention that a brief skim through the various writers" forums will uncover a plethora of general opinions from authors and writing enthusiasts alike, such as this response to a question on Bayt[18]:

> *"Few things can be as frustrating as self-publishing. The chances of (success) for any starting writer is minimal, and even more reduced if he decides to self-publish."*

The Route to Writers' Utopia

As with any polarising subject, for every naysayer, you have the flip side of the coin of people singing its praises. Such as best-selling author and blogger Kristin Lamb who in a blog response[19] to Ros Barber's article:

> *"Self-published authors have largely been responsible for many of the most beneficial changes in publishing history."*

Or novelist Louise Walters who is quoted as saying in an interview with the Guardian newspaper[20]:

> *"Footing the bill to bring out the book means the responsibility is on my shoulders, but at the same time it's incredibly freeing. I can market this book in any*

> *way I choose; I have real input into every decision regarding my work; I'll even earn a fairer share of the proceeds from each sale ... It's only a book, after all, and self-publishing is a whole lot of fun."*

Carlos Harrison quoted Hugh Howey, author of "Wool", in an article in the Miami Herald[21] as saying:

> *"With self-publishing you don't waste your time trying to get published, which can take years of query letters and agenting, and all this stuff. You go straight to the real gatekeepers, which are the readers. If they respond favorably and you have sales, you can leverage that into a writing career. If they don't, you write the next thing. Either way you're not spending your time trying to get published, you're spending your time writing the next work."*

You also find champions of self-publishing in the same authors' forums, such as Olivia Lynn Jormusch and her fantastic response to a Q&A question on Goodreads[22]:

> *"I think self-publishing is a great option for just getting started and building your platform! It helps you walk through the entire process of creating, editing, finishing, publishing, and promoting your book, and you learn SO much through it!"*

The Missing Opinion

One opinion that is suspiciously missing from the debate is that of the big publishing houses. In all my reading on the subject, I have yet to come across a sitting senior exec from any of the big 5 publishers going on record about their views on the boom in self-publishing. My gut feeling is that the Penguin's and the Random House's of the industry either are ignoring it in the hopes that it will go away, which is unlikely. Or they simply are taking the view that is it beneath them to worry about, and if a good book comes out of self-publishing then they could just approach the author directly with a book deal safe in the knowledge that the book has already proven itself. Which is exactly what happened with "50 Shades of Grey", "The Martian", and "The Celestine Prophecy".

My Two Cents

As someone who makes a living helping authors to self-publish, my opinions on the matter should be pretty obvious. But I do agree with some of the points made by those who are fighting against the trend. There ARE loads of poor-quality self-published books out there. Just because you *can* self-publish your book with just a few clicks of a mouse doesn't necessarily mean that you *should*.

I think Louise Walters really hit the nail on the head with her comment about taking responsibility for her book's success. If you truly believe in your book, invest in it! Yes, it is a considerable investment, but it doesn't need to be the extortionate investment that Ros Barber would lead you to believe. Choosing the right editors, designers, and other author support partners is important and can make the difference between your book being a success and you enjoying the process, and you becoming bitter and disillusioned with becoming a writer and giving up on your dream.

In closing I would also like to add that I don't view self-publishing as being black or white; good or bad. I see it as being 50 shades of grey in how appropriate it is for each individual author and their particular situation.

5 Pitfalls of Traditional Publishing: What Every Author Should Know

Traditional publishing has long been the go-to option for authors looking to get their work out to a wide audience. However, while it may seem like the ideal choice, traditional publishing comes with a number of pitfalls that publishers often don't want authors to know about. In this article, we'll explore some of the most significant pitfalls of traditional publishing and discuss why they should be considered before deciding to pursue this path.

Limited Creative Control

One of the biggest pitfalls of traditional publishing is the limited creative control that authors have over their work. When you sign a contract with a publisher, you are essentially giving up control of your book. The publisher may require changes to be made to your manuscript, such as edits to the plot or characters, that you may not agree with. In addition, the publisher may have the final say over the book's cover design and marketing strategy. This can be frustrating for authors who have a specific vision for their work and want to maintain control over it.

Slow Publication Timeline

Traditional publishing is notorious for its slow publication timeline. After a book is accepted by a publisher, it can take up to two years for it to be released to the public. This timeline includes the time it takes for the book to go through editing, design, and printing processes. For authors who are eager to get their work out to readers, this can be a frustratingly long wait.

High Barrier to Entry

Another pitfall of traditional publishing is the high barrier to entry. Publishers typically only accept a small percentage of the manuscripts that are submitted to them. This means that authors must have an exceptional manuscript to even be considered by a publisher. Additionally, authors must have a literary agent to submit their manuscripts to a publisher, and getting an agent can be a difficult process in and of itself.

Limited Royalties

Traditional publishers typically offer authors a royalty rate of 10-15% of the book's retail price. This may sound like a good deal, but it's important to consider the fact that the publisher takes a significant cut of the profits. After accounting for the publisher's share, the author's actual royalty rate may only be a few cents per book sold. This can make it difficult for authors to earn a living solely from their writing.

Limited Marketing Support

Finally, traditional publishers often provide limited marketing support to their authors. While they may send out advance copies to book reviewers and feature the book in their catalogue, they typically don't offer much in the way of advertising or promotional support. This means that authors are often left to do their own marketing and promotion, which can be challenging for those who are new to the publishing world.

In conclusion, while traditional publishing can be a great option for some authors, it's important to consider the pitfalls before deciding to pursue this path. Limited creative control, slow publication timelines, high barriers to entry, limited royalties, and limited marketing support are just a few of the potential pitfalls that authors should be aware of. Ultimately, it's up to each individual author to weigh the pros and cons and decide whether traditional publishing is the right choice for them.

5 Self-Publishing Mistakes & How to Avoid Them

Let's be honest, in the late 2000s self-publishing had a pretty bad reputation. With the introduction of free online self-publishing services like CreateSpace, anyone could publish a book with just a few clicks of the mouse with little thought as to the quality of what they were releasing. The market was suddenly flooded with books that were riddled with mistakes that broke all the cardinal rules that the publishing industry had honoured for over a century.

But times have changed, and independent authors are now starting to understand the value of taking traditional publishing practices and combining them with the agility, control, and ownership that come with self-publishing. So, if you want to self-publish a professional quality book that can compete with traditionally published titles and not get lumped in with all the "bad" self-published books out there, then here are the top 5 self-publishing mistakes that you need to avoid.

1. No Editing

Having your book professionally edited is the golden rule of publishing regardless of whether you are self-publishing or working with a traditional publisher. The majority of readers will not be able to look past poor writing. You could be writing about something that could fundamentally change the readers' life forever, but if your writing is littered with mistakes or doesn't flow very well, you've lost your credibility in your readers' eyes and it's unlikely that they will even finish reading it.

But all editors are not created equal, so don't try to save a bit of money by hiring just any old editor. Editing a book requires a particular set of editing skills that are very different from editing a website or sales copy. To make sure that you are publishing the best version of your book that you can, hire an editor who is a member of the Chartered Institute of Editing & Proofreading (CIEP). CIEP-certified editors must adhere to a set of editorial standards and codes of practice, and you can be assured that they have the training and experience needed to make sure your writing is polished and professional whilst still maintaining your 'voice'.

For more information on the Chartered Institute of Editing & Proofreading, or to search through their director of professional editors, visit https://www.ciep.uk.

2. ISBN Ownership

Another common self-publishing mistake that I see far too many authors make is not being mindful of who owns the ISBN number that is assigned to your book when it's published. As ISBN ownership is not an assertion of copyright, a lot of authors get tempted by online publishing services like Amazon KDP that offer to assign your book a free ISBN as opposed to buying one of their own. The problem with this is that whoever owns the ISBN is listed as the publisher of record for that title. So, if you opted to use the free ISBN offered to you by Amazon KDP (for example), Amazon would be listed as the publisher and NOT you. Kinda defeats the purpose of self-publishing, doesn't it?

Most readers won't notice or care who the listed publisher of a book is, but the trade book industry *does* care. Many retailers will not stock books published by Amazon as they view it as supporting a direct competitor. So, if you don't want your book to be associated with poor-quality self-publishing, then take the time to register your own publishing imprint and purchase your ISBNs. If you're clever about the publishing imprint name that you choose, you can make your book indistinguishable from traditionally published titles. For the sake of £164 (and 20 minutes of your time), it's well worth it.

For more information on ISBNs, check out my article "ISBN Numbers: Everything You Need to Know"

3. Amateur Cover Art

The third common self-publishing mistake I see authors make is not investing in professional cover design.

We've all heard the adage "Don't judge a book by its cover", but as a relatively unknown author, that is exactly what most people will be using to judge whether your book is right for them or not. Think about how you buy books these days… you search Amazon or browse through a particular category. When you see a cover thumbnail or title that piques your interest, you click through to find more information.

If your cover doesn't stand out from the others that it will be listed with, most people won't get to the point of even finding out what your book is about, let alone get a sense of whether it is any good or not. If you want organic sales of your book, you need to have an eye-catching cover that converts. And that takes skill.

The good news is that professional cover design doesn't have to be expensive. I, and many of my clients, use a service called 99 Designs where you can host a design contest for your book cover. For as little as £239 you get dozens of potential designs submitted by reputable and talented cover designers from all over the world for you to choose from.

For more information on 99 Designs and to start your own cover design contest, visit https://99designs.co.uk.

4. Poor Typesetting

Though not as immediately critical as bad cover design, having a badly typeset interior for your book can be just as big a self-publishing mistake. Because most people buy books online now, having an interior that looks like an exported Word document with misaligned margins, a myriad of conflicting fonts, and clipart images that look like they were generated in PowerPoint may not have an immediate effect on the sale for your book, it can have a dramatic effect on the ongoing success of your book.

Think back to when you used to buy books in brick-and-mortar bookstores… when you picked a book up off the shelf, the first thing you did was usually turn it over and if you were intrigued by what you read on the back you'd probably flick through a few pages and possibly look over the table of contents, right? But with online book sales, you don't have the option of doing that. Sure, Amazon does its best to mitigate that by offering its 'Look Inside' feature, but it's not quite the same. (Pro Tip: make sure that your book is compatible with the 'Look Inside' feature on Amazon and enable the feature if you're publishing outside of Amazon… it does make a difference to your sales). So the first opportunity you get to flick through a book is once it arrives in the post.

Some may argue that you've already bought the book by then, so who cares what the inside looks like? But if you flick through a book that you've just spent £10-£15 on and you're a bit disappointed when you first flick through it, you've experienced a negative response to that book before you've ever read a single word of it. Subconsciously that response could colour your impression of the book even after you've read it, and might even prompt you to leave it a negative review… or worse yet, no review at all.

That is the power of professional typesetting. Ensure that your book is judged on the merits of the *content* and not allowing the reader to get distracted by the design (or lack of it). And in today's online consumer market, most products from books to boats live and die by customer reviews and social proof. Make sure that a reader's experience with your book is positive from start to finish and they will reward you by telling other people about it.

5. Limited Distribution

The final self-publishing mistake I see far too many independent authors make is to limit the availability and distribution of their books to just Amazon.

Sure, Amazon is the largest book retailer in the world; you'd be mad to NOT have your book listed on their site. However, you are equally mad to ONLY list your book on their site. Not everyone who actively shops online has an Amazon account. With an increasing backlash against them in the US media, rumours of anti-trust proceedings being brought against them and a growing trend of 'shop local' campaigns, more and more people are looking for alternative retailers to buy from. If your book is not available to buy from where people want to shop, then you are potentially cutting off a percentage of your readership.

Now it used to be those wider distribution models were the sole remit of big publishing houses, but no longer. Self-publishing aggregates like IngramSpark allow for simple worldwide print-on-demand distribution into over 30,000 online retailers across the globe as well as eBook distribution across multiple platforms such as Nook, Kobo and iBooks as well as Kindle.

I also touched on another point of distribution when I discussed ISBNs, and that is that high street brick and mortar book shops will not stock books via Amazon. If you want the overwhelming joy of seeing your book on an actual bookstore bookshelf, then you have to think like a traditional publisher and go wide with your distribution.

To learn more about the wide distribution model and how it relates to self-published books, check out my article "Book Distribution: How to Go Wide".

Conclusion

So there you have it; my list of the top 5 self-publishing mistakes and a brief insight into how you can avoid making them with your next book.

Ultimately, if you want your book to be taken seriously and have the ability to compete with titles published by more traditional publishing houses, then you need to think like a traditional publisher. Invest in professional author services to help you with the things that are not your forte – like editing, design and typesetting. And if you need help to pull it all together or you are feeling a bit overwhelmed by just how much there is to think about, then Book a Call with me. Over a digital coffee, we'll chat about your book and how I can help you avoid all of the mistakes I've just mentioned as well as many more.

Common Self-Publishing Mistakes

There are numerous pitfalls to self-publishing, and many new authors fall into these all errors through ignorance. Just imagine how much easier the publishing process could be if you could avoid these mistakes altogether.

That's the purpose of this article.

People used to say that self-publishing was a waste of time, that self-published books didn't sell and that nobody would take your book seriously unless you were published by a recognised publisher. While this was once true, it is most definitely not the case now. Authors who self-publish correctly, are taken seriously and can have best sellers. The key phrase in the above statement is "when done correctly."

Here is a rundown of the 9 most common self-publishing mistakes I've seen, and a few tips on how you can avoid making them yourself.

Mistake #1: Lack of Clear Purpose

Imagine someone asked you to explain why you were writing your book. How would you respond? What would you say? Your answer to this simple question will have a significant impact on the way you write, design, publish and market your book.

For example, if your answer is *"I just want to capture the family memories of an elderly relative so that future generations of our family can understand what their life was like."* You probably aren't going to worry too much about things like cover design, typesetting and book distribution.

What about If your answer was "*I want to share the story of how I got a degree at age 50 because I want to inspire other older people, who missed out on higher education, to fulfil their lifelong ambition.*"

This answer implies a desire to create a book that will be available to as many people as possible. It also helps to pin down the profile of your target reader. It may give you (or your designer) some clues as to what sort of cover design will be needed to appeal to these people.

How to avoid this mistake
Ask yourself why you are writing your book, and write down notes about your answer. Look back through your notes and pick out any key points that you can use to position your book effectively, and make sure that as you write your book you bear these points in mind. If you've already started writing your book or even finished it, pass these positioning points on to your editor so they can edit your manuscript to fit your positioning as much as possible without compromising the content. More on editors later in this post.

Mistake #2: Failure to Test the Market for Your Book

If your purpose is to create a book that sells, the next question to ask yourself is *"Are there enough people out there who want to buy a book on this topic?"* Many authors assume that there is a market for their book without doing any research to prove it. Such optimism is commendable but usually proves foolhardy. It doesn't take a brain surgeon to work out that if there is no demand, your book won't sell.

How to avoid this mistake
Don't assume there is a market for your book – market testing can save you a lot of time and heartache.

Ideally, you want to "test the water" before expending time and money on self-publishing your book. One way to do this is to tap into the power of your network. Tell your friends, family and existing readers that you are planning to write a book about "X" and ask them if they would be interested in reading a book on that topic. Social Media platforms such as Facebook and Twitter are a great way to test out book ideas before you even put pen to paper.

Another testing option is through your blog. You could write an article based on your book idea, and see what the response is. Share it as widely as possible via email and social media, and then measure the popularity of the article using Google Search Console.

Mistake #3: Starting your book but not finishing it!

Ok so you know why you are writing your book, and you have done your research to prove that there is an audience. The next thing you need to do is knuckle down and write it!

Sadly, I have known many people who repeatedly say that they are going to write a book and then never get around to doing it.

How to avoid this mistake

Set yourself a realistic publication deadline and then draw up a writing schedule that you can stick to.

Your book won't write itself. You'll need to set aside time to outline your ideas, create a structure, and then write the content. Remember, starting your book is relatively easy, finishing it takes stamina, determination and focus. To help you do this, I'll be sharing some proven techniques to help you keep you on track, in a future post.

Next, tell everyone you know about your book and your proposed publishing date. This will help create the motivation you need to get it finished and will give you a level of accountability to help you when your enthusiasm starts to wane.

Mistake #4: Launching without a Marketing Plan

A book without a marketing plan is like a bullet without a gun. Nobody will buy your book if they aren't aware it exists, don't understand what it is about, or don't know why you are uniquely qualified to write it. Marketing is much more than just advertising that your book is available. Amazon is full of amazing self-published books that never sell more than a handful of copies because there is little or no marketing activity behind them.

I often get asked, "When should I start marketing my book?" and my answer is always "Now!" Ideally, you should start promoting your book before it's even been written. Pre-launch marketing creates a tribe of people who are excited about your book and who are hungry to buy a copy when it is published.

How to avoid this mistake

Write out a book-marketing plan and start implementing it as soon as possible. If you don't know how to create your own marketing plan, then find someone who can help. I'll be sharing some practical tips in a future blog post.

Mistake #5: Not getting objective, honest and constructive feedback

Another common self-publishing mistake that new authors make is not to share their first draft with people they trust to give them _honest_, objective feedback. I know, your book is your baby and the thought of having someone criticise it is scary and deeply unpleasant, but trust me, your book will be the better for it. Wouldn't you rather find out any mistakes and shortcomings BEFORE you publish?

A poorly written, hard-to-follow book will do your reputation and credibility much more harm than good.

How to avoid this mistake
Bite the bullet and ask for feedback from people whose opinions your trust and respect. Ideally, you want to do this fairly early in the writing process, and again during editing to ensure you are still on track.

Mistake #6: Doing the Editing and Proofreading Yourself

I've lost count of the number of authors who have chosen to go down the DIY editing and proofreading route to save money, only to realise that it was a false economy. Editing and proofreading are time-consuming tasks that require specialist skills that most authors don't possess.

Look at the acknowledgements page in most bestselling books, and you will see mention of editors and proofreaders. Yes, it costs money to hire these people but think of the time and heartache you save.

How to avoid this mistake
Research editors and proofreaders, and start engaging with the one you like to discuss your book early on in the process. That way you can budget and save for their fees. Follow this one tip, and I guarantee you'll thank me later.

Mistake #7: Doing the Design and Typesetting Yourself

This self-publishing mistake is like the previous one in that it too involves a reluctance on the part of the author to hand over control of their manuscript to a professional, in this case, a designer.

There are three main elements to design work that is always done better by a professional, namely Typesetting, Layout, and Cover Design. There are many reasons why you should avoid this self-publishing pitfall…

1. You're not trained in the art of book layout and are unfamiliar with correct typesetting conventions that will ensure clean, easy-to-read text formatting
2. It is unlikely that you will have the specialist software needed and know how to use it correctly to create a professional-quality file suitable for high-quality print reproduction
3. You aren't a graphic designer and don't have the knowledge and tools to create appropriate supporting graphics such as illustrations, pull quotes or, highlight boxes.
4. You've not been trained in graphic design and don't know how to effectively combine images and colour schemes in the right resolutions and combinations to create a stunning cover that makes your book stand out on the shelf.

How to avoid this mistake

Find a book designer and cover artist who will work with you to turn your precious manuscript into a book that you are proud of and that is appealing to your target buyers. And as with editors, start budgeting for their fees from an early stage.

Mistake #8: Lack of Ongoing Marketing After Launch

This is the final hurdle in turning your book into a best-seller, but many authors ignore this stage altogether. While it's relatively easy to promote your book in the run-up to its launch, it's much harder to maintain that momentum once the euphoria that comes with being a published author dies down.

Ongoing success depends on having a post-launch marketing strategy that keeps driving people to your book's website or sales page, weeks, months, and even years after launch. There are many ways to maintain the sales of your book including; face-to-face networking, speaking engagements, asking readers to post a review, and blogging, podcasting or webinars linked to your book.

How to avoid this mistake

Make sure your marketing plan includes an ongoing programme of promotional activities that extend well beyond your self-published book's launch period. Remember to make sure that all of your activity is coherent and follows the spirit of your book.

Mistake #9: Not Leveraging the Power of Amazon

Amazon is the biggest online book retailer on the planet and, even though it takes quite a significant cut of your sale price, it is simply too big to be ignored. There are several ways that you can benefit from Amazon's sales platform and navigating your way around them can be challenging and bewildering.

Do I sell a paperback edition a Kindle Edition or both? Should I become an Amazon Seller? Should I let Amazon's affiliate print my books or should I use an independent printer? How much should I charge? Which categories should I list my book under?

How to avoid this mistake

Either take the time to learn about the pros and cons of the various Amazon options or find a professional self-publishing manager like me who can advise you on the most appropriate options for your self-publishing goals.

So there you have it. Are you guilty of some of those mistakes? If so, and you want to learn more about how you can avoid them, then get in touch by filling in the contact form at the bottom of the page.

How Long Does it Actually Take to Self-Publish a Competitive Book?

In a number of my recent articles on the blog, I've been talking about the importance and benefits of book planning, and an integral part of a good book plan is a publishing schedule. If you're anything like me, having concrete deadlines helps me keep on track and stay accountable; especially when I'm working on one of my own books as opposed to a client project. But if this is the first time you are publishing a book, how do you know how much time to realistically budget for each stage of the self-publishing process?

So, in this article, I'm going to give you some rough guidelines to work from as to how long each of the 3 main publishing stages should take when done properly.

You may have noticed that in the title of this article, I specified "to Self-Publish a Competitive Book". The reason for this distinction is that in theory, you can publish a book via Amazon KDP in as little as 72 hours. But as with most things, you get out what you put in. To publish a book within three days of writing it means that you are not giving your book enough thought to ensure that it is going to be successful. Remember that you only get one chance to make a first impression. So, if you want your book to make a good impression, you need to give it the time and attention it deserves.

That being said, what attention does it need and how long will that attention to detail take?

Editing – 4 to 10 weeks

Only an author who doesn't really care about the content of their book will publish it without having it properly edited. The amount of time it takes to edit a book manuscript depends on 4 factors:

1. **How long the book is.** This is simple mathematics; it takes less time to edit 10k words than it does to edit 50k words.
2. **The type & complexity of content.** Fiction takes longer to edit than non-fiction. However, non-fiction books that contain a lot of cross-references, copyrighted material, or advanced/technical material will take longer to edit than a straightforward 'how-to' guide or biography.
3. **The level of editing required.** There are three levels of editing that can be performed on your book ranging from simple proofreading on one end of the scale, to line editing as a middle option, and in-depth developmental editing on the other end of the spectrum. Each requires increasing amounts of time to complete.
4. **Editors' workload.** Editors are businesses as well who often have other clients and priorities demanding their attention. They may not be able to start editing your book straight away, or they need to divide their time between you and another author. And because of the level of concentration and skill required to edit a book, many editors will only work on one book at a time.

Scheduling Tip: Send a draft copy of your book (or a couple of chapters) to your chosen editor for them to get a sense of the content and scope of your book, as well as your writing style. From that, they should be able to extrapolate a rough estimate of how long it will take them and the costs to edit your book.

If you need help finding a professional editor, check out the Chartered Institute of Editing and Proofreading (https://www.ciep.uk). They have a searchable directory of all their member editors, plus details of their skills, subject specialisms and services they offer.

Design & Typesetting – 2 to 8 weeks

Despite the old adage, people do judge a book by its cover, so you need to give this its' due attention if you want that judgement to be positive instead of negative. Likewise, how the interior of your book is typeset will have an impact on whether your readers find it easy to read your book or not. Now the amount of time that designing your book cover and typesetting the interior contents takes primarily depends on whether you are doing it yourself or you are hiring professional help.

If you hire a professional designer, this is what a typical book design schedule entails:

- Cover Design
    - Initial concept development – 1 week
    - 2 to 3 rounds of concept proof reviews – 2 to 3 weeks
- Interior Design & Typesetting
    - Initial concept development – 1 week
    - 2 to 3 rounds of concept proof reviews – 2 to 3 weeks
    - Typesetting – 3 to 10 days
    - 2 to 3 rounds of proof reviews – 2 to 3 weeks

*Note that cover design and interior design & typesetting are usually done at the same time.

If you are going to do the design and typesetting of your book yourself, you obviously save yourself time by not needing to do back-and-forth proof reviews, however, you do need to take into account your skill level and learning curve.

Scheduling Tip: I recommend starting your cover design and interior concept development while your editor is working on the initial line edit of your book as this can save you about 4 weeks on your overall schedule.

If you want some more information on the book design process, check out my blog article "The Book Design Process". You might also find "Book

Design Secrets from a Professional Book Designer" and "How to Write a Kick-Ass Book Cover Design Brief" useful.

Publishing – 3 to 6 weeks*

The actual publishing process involves a lot more steps than most first-time authors realise if you want to do it properly. Most of the steps are fairly simple and don't take much time at all but seeing as they need to be done in a particular order, those short amounts of time do start to stack up. Here's a brief outline of the steps involved:

- Registering your publishing Imprint & purchasing ISBN numbers – 1 day
- Drafting your book metadata – 1-2 days
- Setting up publishing accounts with Amazon KDP and Ingram Spark – 1 day
- Submitting your book to Ingram Spark (including Ingram's artwork check) – 3 days
- Ordering a printed test copy for final review – 5-7 days
- Converting approved print book to eBook – 3-5 days
- Submitting an approved print book to Amazon KDP – 1 day
- Submitting converted eBook to Ingram Spark and Amazon KDP – 1 day
- Release for public distribution (including time for book listings to appear across all retail channels) – 3 to 14 days

*Note that this schedule does not include a pre-sale period, which I do recommend that authors include in order to help boost initial Amazon Rankings.

Scheduling Tip: Do NOT rush through drafting your metadata; it is probably the most important step here, and the one that authors often don't give enough thought to. Metadata is how your book actually gets found by people who do not know you or know that you have written a book, so take your time with this step

If you want some more information on what good metadata includes and some advice on how to write quality metadata for your book, check out my blog article "Book Metadata: The Ultimate What, Why & How Guide".

For all you visual people out there, here is what that schedule looks like as a Gantt chart. This is a sample production schedule for an average 50k-word non-fiction book if you were to opt for my All-Inclusive publishing package.

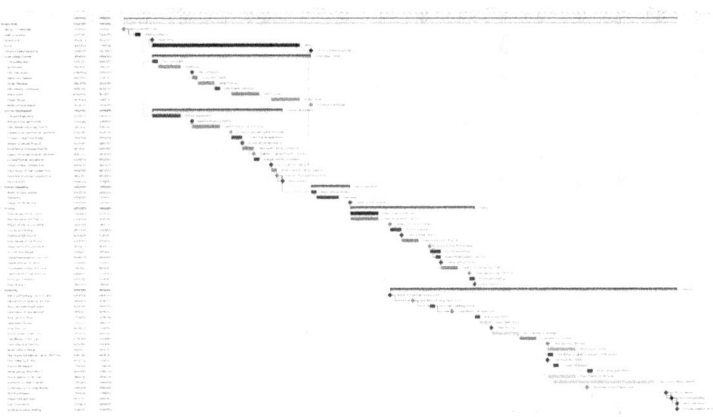

So, there you have it; in 3-4 months you can go from a raw manuscript to a professional quality book available worldwide in both print and eBook. Now that you have an understanding of the steps involved and how long each step can take, you can not only put together a comprehensive publishing plan for your book, but you can also start to be more effective in your marketing by priming your readers with an anticipated release date for your book well in advance.

This system can also be used to reverse engineer a publishing schedule. If you have a particular date that you want your book to be available, you can use this timeline to generate a work-back schedule that gives you dates of when tasks need to be completed in order to hit your publishing deadline.

How Much Should It Cost to Self-Publish Effectively?

I get asked a lot how much it costs to self-publish a book these days, and there are actually several answers. There's the 'technical' answer, there's a minimum answer and there is a recommended answer. In this article, I'm going to explore those different options so that you can put together a *realistic* budget to publish your book based on what you want to get out of it.

The 'Technical' Answer

Technically, you can publish your own book completely for free.

There, I said it… there is nothing stopping you from uploading your manuscript directly to Amazon KDP; using their cover art generator to cobble together a cover, and then having them convert the whole thing to eBook and away you go. BUT… if you actually want to be taken seriously, if you want people to actually pay attention to your book and make a good impression on your readers, **this is the last thing that you should do!!!!!**

I really cannot stress this enough. There is a reason why the phrase "you get what you pay for" exists, and it applies to self-publishing just as much (maybe even more than) everything else to do with your business. If no one can find your book because you didn't give any thought to things like metadata, then the time you spent writing your book was time wasted. If no one buys your book because the cover is clearly clipart or doesn't speak to your audience, the time you spent writing your book was time wasted. If your readers do buy it and then can't see past the spelling, grammar, and continuity errors in it, then they may not even finish your book and will probably give you a bad review. This means the time you spent writing it is more than wasted, it was time spent generating a negative effect on your reputation.

So, though you can technically publish a book without spending a penny, don't! What you have to share with your audience has value – recognise that value and invest in doing it properly.

The 'Minimum' Answer

Now that we've got that out of the way, let's look at what the minimum amount you need to spend on publishing your book should be.

There are two areas that you need to invest in as a bare minimum if you want to publish your book effectively – editing and cover art.

Editing

No matter how good you are at English, no matter how experienced a writer you are, always always ALWAYS hire an editor to review your book. As a bare minimum have them do a proofread to catch the spelling and grammar errors that you will inevitably miss because you are too close to your work. However, I would suggest that you don't stop there and also have them do a full line edit as well. This type of editing goes a bit deeper than just fixing mistakes; it starts to look at how you write and how you get your ideas across. It not only picks up errors with continuity and tense, but it also flags up issues with repetition and potential gaps in your logic or explanations. This is very important for authors who are writing about a subject that they are intimately familiar with for an audience with a much lower level of understanding as what may seem second nature to you may be very complex for a layman.

Think about it… The most famous and successful writers in the world swear by their editors. Whenever they receive prestigious awards for their books, authors will always thank their editors first. This in itself should highlight how important having an editor is to the success of your book.

How Much?

Depending on the skill level of the editor and whether they specialise in your particular subject; expect to pay around £10-£15 per 1k words. Don't be tempted to save money by hiring just any old editor… make sure they have experience in editing books as it takes a more specialist skill set to edit a 50k word book than it does a 1k word article.

Cover Art

The second area that you need to invest in is your book's cover art. The vast majority of book sales these days are made online. Unless someone is looking for your specific book, they will be faced with pages and pages of books to choose from when browsing an online bookstore, and all of those books will initially be presented as tiny thumbnail images. Your book cover has a LOT of work to do to stand out; even in the most niche of categories. Unless you have an understanding of information design, typography, layout and colour psychology, you do not have the necessary skills to ensure that your cover stands out enough to make your reader select your book out of the dozens of others on screen at any one time. And remember that at this stage, they don't have the benefit of seeing a description of what your book is about… all they have is the book title, your name and the cover thumbnail. If you don't catch your readers' attention with those three things, your book will not stand a chance.

How Much?

You've got a bit of flexibility here depending on your budget. You can buy a half-decent cover template that you then edit with your book title and author name for £50-£100 from websites like Envato and GraphicRiver. The downside to using these is that your cover will not be unique to your book. The mid-range option is to use crowdsourcing websites like 99Designs or PeoplePerHour where you can get a cover designed for £150-£250. Generally, these sites will result in a bespoke cover design for your book, but you'll probably be limited on the number of changes you can request from the designer. And of course, you have the high-end option of working one to one with a graphic designer which can cost from £300-£500 for a bespoke cover design where you work directly with a designer to get your perfect cover design exactly how you want it.

The Recommended Answer

Now that we have covered the minimum that you should be investing to publish your book effectively, here are some other areas that I recommend you invest in.

Interior Typesetting

If you really want your book to stand head and shoulders above the crowd, I recommend investing in your interior typesetting. Granted this is an area that will have very little impact on whether a reader buys your book, but it can have a dramatic effect on their impression of your book once they've bought it which can greatly influence whether they recommend your book to others and whether they leave you a good review.

Really good book design is meant to be invisible, which makes it hard to articulate its importance. It's much easier to explain what makes for bad book design. Have you ever tried to read a book and just couldn't concentrate on it… you found your eyes wandering, or you ended up with a headache? There's a very high chance that you were trying to read a book that had been poorly designed. Book design and typesetting ensure that the content of your book is easy to read; that the information is easy to find and presented in a way that is simple to follow.

There are a lot of very minute decisions that go into making that possible. Things like font choice and text size, line length and spacing, heading hierarchy and navigation, colour palette and image treatment, and even the trim size of your finished book. All of these things affect how we read and digest information. Get this wrong and you can inadvertently leave readers with a negative experience of your book even if the content itself is amazing.

How Much?

As with cover design, you have a variety of options depending on your budget and the experience of the designer/typesetter that you work with. Costs can range anywhere between £300 to £2,000+. It is worth noting that there are a lot of variables that go into the cost of typesetting a book such as word count, number of images, and complexity of the design required. I recommend that you work with a designer/typesetter that quotes based on a fixed variable such as word count; that way you know up front how much your book will cost to typeset and is not subject to price changes resulting from fundamental design decisions.

Self-Publishing Management

The final aspect that is worth investing in is self-publishing management; hiring a professional to help you with the actual publishing and book listing process.

It would be a shame for you to invest in all of the above areas of your book to then not have any of your readers be able to find your book because your metadata wasn't optimised, or not able to purchase your book in their country because you have very limited distribution.

A self-publishing consultant can help to make sure that your book listing is optimised with the best keywords to make your book appears when your readers search for your topic. They can help you determine the most competitive categories to list your book under to help your book rank better and appear top of the list when readers are browsing for particular genres. And most importantly, they can help make sure that the metadata that sits behind your book listing is as complete as possible making it easier for physical bookstores, libraries and distributors to find out about your book in order to further widen your books' reach.

How Much?

This is a fairly new author service that very few companies are providing as a stand-alone service – it is usually bundled into a complete publishing package, so finding comparison data is a bit tricky. But from the very few examples that I could find, you're looking at between £500-£800.

A word of caution here… with any self-publishing service (whether it's just publishing consultation or full-service packages that I will mention below) make sure that you own your ISBN number; even if it means paying a little bit extra. The benefits far outweigh the additional cost. If you want to find out why, check out my blog post on ISBN numbers here.

The All-Inclusive Answer

I appreciate that this is all a lot to take in, and lots of various things to think about and different services to source on your own. That is why I recommend an all-inclusive package solution. This is where you work with one self-publishing consultant or publishing service provider and they arrange all of the various services that you will need including editors, cover designers, and typesetters and they will manage the process of actually getting your book published.

There are some things you need to make sure of when you're considering using one of these services. First, make sure that YOU are going to be listed as the publisher of your book. There are a lot of online services professing to help authors with self-publishing when they are actually offering hybrid publishing in which you have many of the same trappings of a traditional publishing deal, but you are paying for the privilege of not having to go through a submissions process.

Also, make sure that any contractual agreement you sign includes the following:

- you will own the rights to all artwork
- that ISBN numbers will be purchased in your name
- that you will be given all final artwork files
- that you will have access to self-publishing accounts
- that the service will not take any residual royalties once the book is published

How Much?

Costs for all-inclusive packages can vary wildly from £2,500-£8,000 depending on word count and what additional services are included such as author copies and book marketing add-ons.

If you opt to work with me at SWATT Books, my all-inclusive publishing package is **£3,800** for a 50k word non-fiction book and **£3,900** for a 90k word novel. Both packages include:

- Professional editing & proofreading
- Bespoke cover design with full ownership rights
- Bespoke interior design and typesetting
- Conversion of the print edition to EPUB for publishing to Kindle, Nook, Kobo, and iBooks
- Registration of your publishing imprint in your name and purchase of your ISBN numbers so you own 100% of the rights
- Set up publishing accounts with KDP (for Amazon), and IngramSpark (for international distribution) in your name so you keep 100% of your royalties
- Fully facilitated publishing of your book on all major Amazon sites as well as 7,000 online book retailers worldwide (including Barnes & Nobel, Chapters/Indigo, Waterstones, The Book Depository, and more)
- Submission of title details to the International ISBN Database, and fulfilment of Legal Deposit requirements
- Access to my extended network of author services to help you with any part of your publishing journey (including marketing & PR agencies, audiobook studios, writing mentors, and more)

To find out more about working with me or to discuss publishing your own book, click here to book a no-obligation 1hr consultation with me.

What NOT to Spend Money On

One last point on what you should NOT be spending money on when publishing your book, and rather counterintuitively that's printing.

With print-on-demand technology being so readily available and of such high quality, long gone are the days when you would take your book to a traditional litho printer to have a bulk print run of 500-1,000 copies produced in the *hopes* that you would sell them all.

Traditional printing obviously has its place in the publishing world, however, for a first-time author it is too much of a risk and requires too much in the way of logistics to manage effectively. Using print-on-demand technology to produce your book eliminates the risk of being stuck with hundreds of books that you need to store for months and often years. It also alleviates the necessity for finding distribution partners to get your books from your storage to retailers to your readers.

Yes, PoD printing does have its drawbacks such as limitations on print specifications and slightly higher per-unit costs. However, the benefits for authors just finding their feet with publishing far outweigh the restrictions and the time and hassle saved in not having to worry about distribution more than pays for any cost differences.

I hope that has demystified what the cost of self-publishing a book effectively should be. If you have any questions, please do pop them in the comments or book a consultation with me here and we can chat about your specific publishing project.

What Is Self-Publishing Management

Over the past few weeks since officially launching my self-publishing management service, I've had a number of people ask me what it is and what the difference is between what I offer and either doing it themselves or going down the route of traditional publishing. So in this post I'm going to explain what self-publishing management is and isn't, and list some of the comparisons between the 3 main publishing options available to you.

What Self-Publishing Management is NOT

It will be easier to start out with what self-publishing management is not, rather than what it is. Self-publishing management is not like traditional publishing; there are no gatekeepers who arbitrarily decide whether your book is worthy of publishing that you need to convince to take on your book and then pay a handsome percentage of your royalties to for the privilege. On the flip side of that coin, there are also no teams of editors and PR gurus to polish your book and its launch plan until it shines like the shiny new penny that it is (though there is nothing stopping you from hiring these professional polishers yourself; in fact I recommend it!).

Self-publishing management is also not the lonely, isolated, and frustrating road to publishing solo; with no one to guide you in the right direction, to offer advice on the business aspects of your book, or to help you wade through the myriad options available when self-publishing.

What Self-Publishing Management IS

Self-publishing management is the happy halfway house between the two extremes of traditional publishing and self-publishing solo. You get the freedom to decide your books' own destiny and to keep 100% of the royalties for all your hard work. You also get the support of an experienced self-publishing manager to help you every step of the way from deciding on what format your book should take, to help you determine pricing and wholesale discounts, to actually doing the legwork of getting your book printed, published, and selling on Amazon.

Think of me as your publishing PA; it's still your book with your name or imprint as the publisher and it's still you who ultimately shoulders the responsibility of whether or not your book succeeds. However, I am here to manage all of the waypoints along the journey that your book needs to take from manuscript to published work; making sure it's as enjoyable and profitable an experience for you as possible.

How Self-Publishing Management Fits Into The Publishing Landscape

I'm going to conclude with a quick comparison matrix between the three main publishing options that are available today. There are of course numerous book and publishing agencies that blur the lines between these three categories, but they are the main ones:

Publishing Options Comparison

Aspect	Traditional Publishing	Self-Publishing Management	Solo Self-Publishing
Gatekeepers who decide whether your book gets published	Yes	No	No
Who has ultimate creative control	They do, with your input	You do	You do

Publishing Options Comparison

Aspect	Traditional Publishing	Self-Publishing Management	Solo Self-Publishing
Do you get editorial support	Yes	Assistance available	No
Do you get PR & Marketing support	Yes	Assistance available	No
Who does the actual publishing work	They do	They do	You do
Who manages printing	They do	They do	You do
Who holds ownership of the final book	You retain intellectual copyright, but they own the book	You do	You do
Is there a contract to sign	Yes; usually a fixed term with obligations to fulfil	No	No
How much of your Royalties do you keep	Percentage	All	All
Who pays the publishing costs	They do	You do	You do
Cost of using the service	No, they pay you	Yes, usually one off with option for monthly ongoing management	No

5 Self-Publishing Resources You Need to Publish a Quality Book

There are loads of self-publishing resources available online to help authors through the oftentimes confusing and overwhelming journey of independent publishing. Everything you can think of from artwork generation to marketing, distribution to advice and top tips. Some are free; others can be quite expensive. Some are a bit frivolous and gimmicky, but some are essential if you want to do things properly and give your book the best chance of competing against titles from the big publishing houses.

Here is my list of the top 5 self-publishing resources you need if you want to publish a professional-quality book that has the best chance of success.

Self-Publishing Resource #1: CIEP

The Chartered Institute of Editing and Proofreading (CIEP), which was formerly the Society for Editors and Proofreaders (SfEP), is a non-profit professional accreditation body that promotes excellence in English language editing. If you are looking for a professional editor for your book that you can trust and who knows what they are doing (which is a MUST if you want to publish a quality book), this is the place to find them.

The CIEP maintains a directory of over 700 CIEP members which is searchable by skills, subjects or services offered. For an editor to become a CIEP member, they must adhere to a strict Code of Practice and have demonstrated a certain level of editorial skill through continued professional development, training and tests.

To find out more visit https://www.ciep.uk.

Self-Publishing Resource #2: 99Designs

To give your book the best chance of success, it needs a stellar cover design. The problem is that many professional graphic design agencies are expensive; often more expensive than what a first-time author can afford. That's where 99Designs comes in.

99D is a global creative platform that connects talented freelance designers with anyone who needs great creative work. They do this through a curated contest model that gives you access to lots of creative ideas and interpretations of your cover art for a single low-cost fee. Designers pitch their ideas to you, and the winner gets the fee.

I have been using this platform of nearly all of my clients' covers as well as the cover art for my own books for several years now and would not look to change anytime soon. The contest model means that you get more than one designer's interpretation of your cover, and I have not once had any problems with the artwork quality or professionalism of the artists who produce them.

Book cover contests start at £168 for a paperback. You can opt for higher reward contests which will attract more designers to participate, but I've traditionally received between 30-50 concepts from an entry-level contest.

99D isn't just for cover art either. If you need help with interior design and typesetting, or the production of any marketing material (such as bookmarks, author website, etc.), they have categories of contests for pretty much every conceivable design requirement.

To find out more visit https://99designs.co.uk.

Self-Publishing Resource #3: Your Own Publishing Imprint

To demonstrate that you mean business as a credible independent author, you need to publish your book (s) using ISBNs that you own. To be able to purchase those ISBNs, you need to register your own publishing imprint with the ISBN agency for your territory; in the UK and Ireland, that agency is Nielsen Book Services.

I have a whole article that talks about what ISBNs are, what they are used for, and why it is so important that you use ISBNs that you own. You can read that article here, but the long and short of it is that an ISBN allows your book to be sold through a retail channel (like Amazon or Waterstones) and facilitates sales tracking and wholesale ordering of your book. It also gives you a certain amount of control over what happens with your book in those retail environments, so don't be fooled by online self-publishing services offering to give you a free ISBN as part of their package – it's a false economy.

To find out more about registering your publishing imprint with Nielsen's visit https://nielsenbook.co.uk/isbn-agency/, or to find out more about ISBNs in general visit the International ISBN Agency which regulates the worldwide use of the ISBN system at https://www.isbn-international.org.

Self-Publishing Resource #4: Your Own PoD Publishing Accounts

Book distribution is another area that can make or break a book's success. It is quite feasible to manage all the distribution of your book yourself, but it can be very time-consuming and requires you to have a good head for logistics and sales. But if you want to compete with titles from the big publishers, you need to make sure your book is available in all the same retailers that they are. That level of distribution is now available to the independent author thanks to professional-grade print-on-demand publishing platforms.

To ensure the widest distribution for your book possible, you want to have publishing accounts with IngramSpark and Amazon KDP and replicate your book listing on both platforms. This ensures that your book is available on all major Amazon sites as well as over 30,000 online book retailers, universities and libraries around the world. I go into more detail on the topic of 'going wide' with y our book distribution in another blog post that I published last month, which you can read here.

To find out more about IngramSpark visit http://www.ingramspark.com, and for Amazon KDP visit https://kdp.amazon.com/en_US/.

Self-Publishing Resource #5: An International ISBN Database listing

The last of my self-publishing resources that you need is an extension of your publishing imprint and ISBNs, and that's a means of submitting your books' metadata to the International ISBN Database. This is a database that each territorial ISBN agency maintains that holds a record of all of the books that have been published within that territory.

The reason why this database is important is that many book retailers, especially physical brick-and-mortar bookstores, use this database as a catalogue of books that are available for them to stock. Shops like Waterstones rely solely on this database for their stock ordering process and they will not sell a book in their stores that is not listed in the ISBN Database.

Many territories such as the United States and Australia combine their database listing process with the imprint registration and ISBN purchasing process. However, Nielsen has opted to keep these two services separate in the UK. To submit your books' metadata for inclusion in the ISBN Database, you will need a Nielsen Title Editor account.

A Title Editor account is free to set up, but it does take a couple of weeks to process, so be sure to sign up for an account as soon as you have registered your publishing imprint and purchased your ISBNs.

To find out more about Nielsen Title Editor, visit https://www.nielsentitleeditor.com/titleeditor/.

Conclusion

So that's it, my list of the top 5 self-publishing resources you absolutely need in order to publish a quality book. If you utilise these 5 resources, you will be giving your book the best chance of success and the ability to compete side-by-side with titles from any of the big publishing houses.

Do you have any self-publishing resources that you find invaluable? Let us know in the comments.

Book Metadata: The Ultimate What, Why & How Guide

Book metadata is a vitally essential ingredient in book marketing and discoverability. If you are a relatively unknown author, then producing good-quality metadata is just as important as producing a good-quality book. Without it, your book will languish in obscurity, no matter how great it may be in every other regard. But what IS book metadata, and how do you best use it to your advantage to publish a successful book? This ultimate guide is going to look at what book metadata is, why it's so important, and give you some practical tips on how to best put metadata to work promoting your book.

So, let's start at the beginning and answer the burning question of what the heck is book metadata.

What is Book Metadata?

Book metadata is what distinguishes your book from everybody else's and any other book(s) you might publish in the future. As a whole, book metadata covers a vast array of nearly 4,000 individual data points ranging from various types of classification, contributor information, content descriptors, and specifications. Thankfully, there is a huge difference between the amount of metadata you *can* create versus the amount of metadata you *should* create, as illustrated in this graphic from "Metadata Essentials" by Jake Handy and Margaret Harrison.

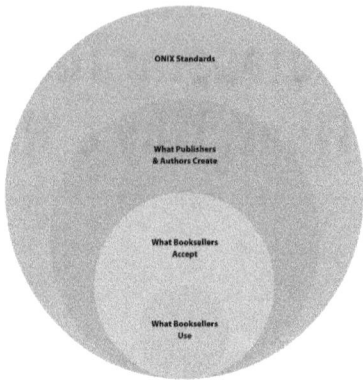

As for where book metadata sits in the grand scheme of things, it acts as a filter between what you as the author/publisher (as well as any aggregators or distributors that you use in getting your book to market) create and what consumer-facing channels such as retailers and libraries present to their users (both online and offline) to help them make buying decisions.

Why is Book Metadata So Important?

In this current day and age where the majority of books are sold online, metadata acts as a means of bringing your book to life and allowing potential readers to better judge whether your book is right for them.

Think back to the last time you went to a library or a physical bookstore looking for your next read. You would have had the opportunity to walk up and down the aisles, stopping at genre sections that you had an interest in and browsing through the book jackets looking for something that piqued your curiosity. You'd then pick a book up off the shelf and read the back cover blurb and maybe the author bio; you might have even flicked through some of the pages and glanced at the table of contents if it was non-fiction – just to make sure you were getting the information you wanted.

Now compare that experience with shopping for a book online. You don't get any of those interactions with a book before you buy it. That's where book metadata comes in. Really good metadata answers all of the questions that you are subconsciously asking when you perform all those little tasks in a bookstore or library when deciding what book to buy. It helps the reader to anticipate what he or she should expect when they receive your book in the mail.

How Book Metadata Works

When it comes to selling books online, book metadata and discoverability go hand in hand. To the average self-published author, metadata works in the same way that SEO does for a website; it enables people who have not heard of you or your book to learn about your book's existence and then help them decide whether your book is right for them. To understand how book metadata works, you need to have a basic understanding of how book search engines, like those used on Amazon, work.

Amazon employs an automated search algorithm, similar to that used by Google, called A9. However, unlike Google's algorithm which is designed to provide the most accurate answer to a question, A9 is designed specifically to provide the best product for a situation and ultimately to make you buy as much as possible. As such, an Amazon search will not only bring up products that are relevant to your search but will also rank those products according to what it thinks you are most likely to buy based on several different factors such as click-through rate, conversion rate, overall sales, and keyword relevance. Because Amazon's ultimate goal is to make as much revenue as possible (not only short term, but long term as well), they not only want you to buy, but they want to make sure that you will be satisfied with your purchase so that you will come back. As such A9 also takes into account other factors that algorithms like Google don't such as reader reviews, product image quality, bestseller status, and participation in Amazon features (i.e. Look Inside, Kindle Unlimited, and other Amazon programs).

It's important to understand that an automated algorithm like A9 is a distillation of all of these factors combined, so you won't always see a direct correlation between changes to your metadata and your Amazon search rankings. But by familiarizing yourself with these factors and applying best-practice techniques to the book metadata that you produce; you will give yourself the best chance of increasing your books' SEO and potential sales.

That being said, one of the most important ways that you boost your books' SEO is to create great metadata that contributes to click-through rate and ultimately to sales. So, without any further ado, let's take a look at the essential book metadata that you should include with every title you publish and give you some pointers on how to maximise each metadata field.

Book Metadata Essentials

Remember how I mentioned earlier that there are nearly 4,000 potential data points that you *could* include in a book metadata set? Well, to make things easier for you, here is a list of the metadata elements that your book should NOT leave home without. Nail these, and you're well on your way to giving your book the best chance at success.

1. Title, Subtitle & Edition
2. Contributors
3. Contributor Bio
4. Series (if applicable)
5. Description
6. Category & Subject Codes (aka Genre)
7. Keywords
8. Format
9. Review Quotes
10. Audience Code
11. Age Range (if applicable)

Let's look at each data point individually in more detail…

Title, Subtitle & Edition

A book's title is your first chance to make an impression on your reader, so be sure to give careful consideration to the title you choose. Some authors make the mistake of thinking that if they title their book similarly to another more famous title it will help improve discovery, but this is not the case – your book will get buried below the more famous versions and readers will potentially miss your book completely. So be sure that your title is as distinct and unique to your book as possible.

If the title you wish to use is a bit close to the title of another publication or book, then use the Subtitle field to add distinction. A subtitle should add clarity to the main title but should always be listed as a separate data point – never combine them, even if they appear together on your cover artwork. It is also good practice to include relevant keywords in your subtitle if possible but avoid forcing keywords (also known as keyword stuffing) simply for the sake of SEO as it could confuse your reader. It is also worth pointing out to not include any series names in the subtitle field if your book is part of a series; this has its own metadata field that is separate which we will cover shortly.

Lastly, if the book you are publishing is an update on a previously published title, then be sure to include edition information. This ensures that readers are aware of which is the most current version and what has potentially changed from the last edition. The Edition metadata set includes the Edition number, Edition type and Edition description.

Pro Tip: Keep your title to fewer than 80 characters (including subtitles) so that it's optimised for mobile browsing.

Contributors

Including a detailed Contributor section in your book metadata allows for a more immersive and interlinked search experience for your readers. Not only can they then find other books that you have published or been involved with, but they can also find books relating to other contributors involved in your book. For example, if a reader loves the illustrations you used in your book and you included your illustrator's details as a contributor, that reader can then find other books illustrated by that same artist. Because of this, retailers like Amazon love to see a more robust contributor dataset than just author names.

In addition to simply listing all of the contributors to your book by first and last name and by the role they played in your book (i.e. author, illustrated by, edited by, cover designed by, etc.), it is also beneficial to include location data for each contributor so that readers can then find titles by local authors.

Pro Tip: Be sure to include all of the names from the cover or title page and be consistent with spelling and presentation (for example J.R.R. Tolkien or Dr. Rangan Chatterjee).

Contributor Bio

A contributor biography is recommended for all listed contributors but should be considered essential for the author and any co-authors. These biographies are frequently shown on retail listings to provide readers with a bit of background on the author and to make them more relatable. A good biography should be brief but packed with notable facts and achievements such as relative credentials or experience, prior work or awards, related associations or affiliations, and any other activities and information that a potential reader may find interesting.

It is recommended to use HTML markup in your biography to highlight important points or works for the reader. You can include website addresses for the reader to conduct more research should they wish, but you want to avoid including any active hyperlinks to those websites that might tempt readers to click away from your book listing.

Pro Tip: Keep biographies between 50 and 250 words for each contributor and avoid using external links such as blogs or author websites (you don't want to pull potential buyers away from buying your book).

Series (if applicable)

If your book is part of a series, then it is imperative to inform the reader of that fact by listing the series name and number as part of your book metadata. These details can be added retrospectively if you publish a book with the intention of it being a standalone work, but then add other titles to the series in the future.

It is also important to include the series number for each book where the order in which the books within the series are to be read is important (for example with fictional trilogies). However, if the order of books within a series is not meaningful, then this dataset can be left blank.

Just as the subtitle should never be included in the title field, the series name and number should never be included in the subtitle field.

Pro Tip: If your book is part of a series, then be sure to tell your readers about it every chance you get. If they enjoy the first book; they'll want to buy the rest.

Description

Consisting of both a long and short version, your book description should be an accurate, compelling and comprehensive breakdown of what a reader can expect when they buy your book. Here's a brief anatomy of what makes a great book description:

Headline – start with a bold first line. Make it punchy and attention-grabbing. This is the basic elevator pitch for your book and is critical for SEO. It also acts to hook a potential buyer into reading more.

Exposition – This is the meat of your description consisting of one to two paragraphs giving buyers the information they need to make an informed decision as to whether your book is right for them. Include things like who or what the book is about, where and when the is story set, and what happens.

Close – this is your persuasive "why to buy" paragraph. Keep it short and sweet and emphasise the value that your book provides. Focus on what they will get out of reading it and why they should buy it now.

The short description should be a single paragraph distillation of all of the above condensed into 150-200 words.

It is worth mentioning that it is very rare for a short and long description to appear side by side, but instead work in tandem at various points of the buying journey. As such they should be written to complement each other.

Pro Tip: Describe your book in a conversational tone but keep it to between 200-600 words. A bold opening line and paragraph breaks (coded using HTML) work best to grab attention.

Category & Subject Codes (aka Genre)

Category and Subject codes indicate to potential buyers, retailers and search engines what your book is actually about – the genre, topic or theme that your book covers. Unfortunately, despite being one of the most important data points to help potential readers organically find your book, it is also the most complicated and confusing to get right because there isn't one all-encompassing system or standard that is used across the whole of the industry.

The most commonly used set of subject codes is BISAC (Book Industry Standards and Communications). It has the widest range of codes available and hundreds of new codes are added to the list each year. You can view the full list at https://bisg.org/page/BISACEdition. However, Amazon and Walmart (two of the largest book retailers in the world) use their own proprietary subject schema, so you see what I mean about confusing and complicated.

So, in the hopes of simplifying things a bit for you, here is some best-practice advice:

- Chose one BISAC code as a minimum, but three is considered best to help ensure the broadest reach for your book
- Order those three codes by the most relevant and important first
- Avoid using general codes if a more specific or granular code is available
- Chose subject codes from multiple top-level headings if at all possible, to broaden discoverability

If you want to get a little bit more advanced, or if your book is intended for an international audience, then you can supplement your BISAC codes by adding in additional Thema codes. Thema is a fairly new coding system that replaced the BIC category codes in 2017. It is still in its infancy with only about 29% of retailers using it, but it is growing in popularity. Its biggest benefit is that it was developed for international use as opposed to BISAC which is more North American-biased. Thema schemes can provide an extremely precise subject code as it is broken down into subject categories and qualifiers including national extensions. To find out more about Thema, visit https://www.editeur.org/151/Thema/.

Pro Tip: Choose 2-3 highly specific categories using the BISAC subject code system. If you don't find exactly what you need, then supplement using keywords.

Keywords

The use of keywords in your book metadata improves online retail categorisation and search engine optimisation by aligning your book with how consumers use the internet to search for things. While not all retailers actively use keywords in their online systems, Amazon certainly does, so it is worth your while to spend time on this section.

When developing the keywords for your book, always put yourself in your readers' shoes. How would they describe your book? What topics do they care about? What words and phrases might they type into Google to find information on those topics? Keywords should be used in a way that most effectively helps a potential buyer to find your particular book, so in short, the more specific the better.

Some other best-practice advice on keywords includes:

- Don't waste keywords on the author, title, contributors, or other defined metadata points – they're already searchable
- Use at least 7 keyword phrases, separated by a semicolon and no space
- Do not include any quotation marks around keywords
- Put the most relevant and important keywords first
- Use keyword phrases that complement (but don't replicate) the book description
- The most useful keyword types to consider are:
    - Specific topics that do not have an equivalent BISAC code
    - Core topics and themes

- Locations and/or time periods
- Story tone and/or writing style
- Character types and roles
- Format or audience notes

Pro Tip: Have a MINIMUM of 5-7 keywords or phrases that your reader would actually use and incorporate them throughout your metadata as well as in the specific keyword metadata field.

Format

Format (or product form) data details the technical specifications of your book so that readers know what to expect to receive when they buy your book. Are they going to get a paperback or a hardback, if it's an eBook is it going to come as an EPUB or a MOBI file? This is the most basic level of metadata and generally a minimum requirement for both physical and digital books.

If you are publishing a physical product, this data also includes information about the accurate size and weight of the book to aid in purchasing, inventory management and merchandising decisions on behalf of the retailer. Measurements should include height, width, depth (or page count) and weight, and should be provided as a decimal figure (do not use fractions, even if you are providing measurements in inches).

Pro Tip: Choose the format that is most descriptive of your binding type, such as mass-market paperback or EPUB eBook. Also, be sure to use a unique ISBN number for each format.

Review Quotes

Including review quotes as part of your book metadata is not a requirement by any retailer, but it is highly recommended that if you have any positive reviews from beta readers or ARC's (advance reader copies), that you include them in your metadata at the point of publication. This acts to provide social proof to potential buyers before your book has had a chance to collect reviews submitted by readers.

Pro Tip: Include 2 to 8 positive review quotes from industry sources, publications and relevant people such as other authors and influencers within your genre or industry.

Audience Code

The audience code is used to help potential buyers and retailers assign a broad audience demographic to your book. Always aim to use the correct and specific audience code that best describes your primary audience.

There are two categories of audience code: Trade/consumer and Specialty. Trade/consumer audiences consist of General/trade for general adult audiences, Children/juvenile for general children's audiences not related to any specific educational purpose, and Young adult for young and adult and teen audiences again not related to any particular educational purpose. The Specialty audience codes deal more with educational levels such as primary, secondary, elementary, high school, college or general higher education, and professional and scholarly subjects which also include adult education and second-language teaching.

Pro Tip: Choosing the correct audience code ensures that your title will be merchandised correctly (i.e. general adult, juvenile or young adult). Also, make sure that your subject codes and audience codes coincide (i.e. young adult audience code with a young adult subject code).

Age Range (if applicable)

The audience age range data points are intended to narrow down the audience demographic even further. Age range is a mandatory field for either of the children's or young adult audience codes. It is also recommended to include an age range for mature graphic novels and other similar works that might be easily confused as children's titles.

The age range that you choose should be both realistic and as specific as possible – ideally to a 2-year range for children and a 4-year range for young adults. Your potential buyers will be using this data to determine whether your book is suitable for their children.

Pro Tip: If you chose a juvenile or young adult audience code, pick a more specific age or grade range to target. Use a 2-year age/grade range for children and a 4-year age/grade range for young adults.

Book Metadata and IDs

I can very much appreciate that when you look at all the various data points that are included in a robust set of book metadata, it can be very overwhelming. Especially when you start looking at associating contributors from one title with another and relating individual books with other titles, it can all get very messy very quickly. That's where the final, overarching data point you need to include in your metadata comes in… Identification codes – in particular ISBN numbers.

ISBN numbers are essential for any publication regardless of format. It provides the underlying identification for a title within both internal catalogues and external services such as retailers and libraries. Without it, your book cannot be distributed and sold via retail channels; the sales of those books cannot be tracked, and your book could become entangled and confused with numerous other books with similar titles or other metadata entries.

For more information on ISBN numbers, please see my blog post "ISBN Numbers: Everything You Need to Know" (https://swatt-books.co.uk/isbn-numbers-everything-you-need-to-know).

Conclusion

So, there you have it. A bit longer than my normal posts, but hopefully, you will find the information helpful when it comes to putting together the metadata for your next book. If you want to learn more about book metadata and get more specific tips and advice, then check out "Metadata Essentials" by Jake Handy and Margaret Harrison; published by Ingram Publisher Services (available on Amazon).

Cracking the Code: How to Choose the Best Category for Your Book on Amazon

When it comes to selling a book on Amazon, one of the most important decisions you will make is choosing the right category to list it in. The category you choose can greatly impact the visibility and sales of your book, so it's important to take the time to research and choose the best category for your book. In this article, we will discuss some tips to help you decide which category to list your book in on Amazon.

Why Amazon category choice is important

Your choice of Amazon category is very important for two main reasons:

1. Searchability
2. Amazon Sales Ranking

Searchability

Choosing the right category on Amazon can significantly influence the searchability of your book on Amazon. When users search for books on Amazon, they often use specific keywords and phrases related to the topic they're interested in. By choosing the right category, your book will be more visible to users searching for specific keywords related to your book. For instance, if your book is about vegan cooking, listing it in the Cooking, Food & Wine category or the Vegan & Vegetarian Cooking sub-category can help it appear in front of users searching for these specific keywords. Therefore, by carefully selecting the right category for your book, you can improve its searchability on Amazon, making it more discoverable to potential readers and increasing the chances of driving more sales.

Amazon Sales Ranking

The category you choose for your book on Amazon can also have a substantial impact on your book's Amazon Sales Rankings. When you list your book in a category, Amazon's algorithm places your book in a sales ranking for that specific category. This means that if you choose a highly competitive category, it can be more challenging to rank high on the sales chart. In contrast, if you choose a less competitive category, you may have a higher chance of ranking high on the sales chart. Therefore, it's essential to select the right category for your book to increase its visibility and sales. The right category can help your book appear in front of your target audience, leading to more sales and higher rankings on Amazon.

How to choose your Amazon category

Now that we know why choosing the right category for your book is so important, let's take a look at what you should consider when deciding which category or categories to list your book under.

1. Research your genre

Before you start listing your book, research your genre and subgenre to identify the categories where your book might fit. Start by looking at the books that are similar to yours, and see what categories they are listed in. Look at the top-selling books in your genre to get an idea of what categories are popular and which ones might be more competitive.

2. Consider the audience

Think about who your target audience is and what categories they might be looking for. If your book is a self-help book for women, for example, you might consider listing it in the Women's Studies category. If your book is a mystery novel, you might consider listing it in the Mystery, Thriller, and Suspense category.

3. Look at the competition

Look at the books that are currently bestsellers in your chosen categories, and see how your book stacks up against them. Are there a lot of books in the category? Are there any gaps in the market that your book could fill? Is your book more or less specific than the books that are currently listed in the category?

4. Consider the sub-categories

Amazon has a lot of sub-categories, and it's important to consider which ones might be a good fit for your book. For example, if you're listing a book about healthy eating, you might consider listing it in the Cooking, Food & Wine category, but you could also list it in sub-categories like Nutrition, Diets & Weight Loss, or Special Diet Cooking.

5. Think about keywords

Keywords are important for discoverability on Amazon, so consider the keywords that readers might use to search for books like yours. Make sure to include these keywords in your book description and also consider listing your book in categories that include these keywords.

6. Be strategic

Sometimes it can be a good idea to list your book in a less competitive category to increase visibility and sales. For example, if you have a book about entrepreneurship, you might consider listing it in the Small Business & Entrepreneurship category rather than the more competitive Business & Money category.

In conclusion, choosing the right category to list your book in on Amazon is an important decision that can greatly impact the success of your book. By researching your genre, considering your audience, looking at the competition, considering sub-categories, thinking about keywords, and being strategic, you can choose the best category to increase your book's visibility and sales.

3 Factors to Consider When Setting an Attractive Cover Price

Sticking with our theme on the blog this month, let's talk about another big financial decision you need to make to make your self-published book a success – setting an attractive cover price.

The cover price of your book is one of the key components that determine how much royalty you will earn when you sell a copy – either through a retail channel like Amazon or Waterstones or direct to a reader. Set your cover price too high and you could price yourself out of the market; set it too low and you could damage your profitability. A fine line to walk.

In this post, we're going to look at the 4 main factors that you need to consider to set an attractive cover price that will ensure both happy readers and a happy bank balance.

Factor 1: Print Cost

The first main aspect that you need to factor into setting an attractive cover price is how much it will cost to get each copy of your book printed. This is a fixed cost at is determined by the physical specifications of your book such as trim size, binding type, page count, and whether the interior pages are printed in full colour or black and white.

If you are publishing your book via print-on-demand platforms such as IngramSpark or Amazon KDP, you will be told exactly what the price cost of each copy is when you submit your book listing. Ingram also has a very helpful set of free online calculators to help you experiment to find the optimum specifications for your book before you commit to generating book artwork. The Print & Ship Calculator (https://myaccount.ingramspark.com/Portal/Tools/ShippingCalculator) helps you work out how much it will cost to get books printed and sent to you. The Publishers Compensation Calculator does give you the cost of printing for a book to be sent to a retailer, but is primarily for working out your anticipated royalty – which will come in handy later on…

If you decide to publish your book using a self-distribution model where you get a stock of books printed by a traditional printer and then distribute them yourself, you will need to start getting some quotes from printers. In this scenario, the more books you order, the cheaper the cost of each book but don't be fooled as this can be a false economy. You will need to take into consideration the cost to store these books while they are waiting to be sold, as well as the cost of shipping them either to a retailer or to the end consumer. A good rule of thumb for calculating individual book production costs in a self-fulfilment publishing model is to take the total cost of your print order, plus any storage costs for 3 months; divide by the number of books you get printed, and then add the courier cost of shipping one book to a consumer.

Once you know your book production cost, you need to make sure that the cover price is the same price or higher. If it isn't, your book will never pay for itself, and you will lose money on every copy sold.

Factor 2: Market Averages

The next factor to consider when setting an attractive cover price is what the market averages for other books similar to yours. The easiest way to do this is to go onto Amazon and browse through the book category in which you will be published into. First, look for your closest competitors and make a note of their retail prices. Next, make a note of the retail prices for the top 10 bestselling books in that category. Once you have a list of 10-15 books, highlight the most expensive and cheapest, then calculate the average.

A couple of things to note during this exercise… Be sure to only note down the full RRP and not the price that Amazon is selling it for as Amazon quiet often discounts books. Also, be mindful of the print specifications of the books that you are looking at. Make sure that they are a similar binding type and page count to yours. A 200-page hardback is going to have a dramatically different cover price to a 100-page paperback.

Once done, you will have a maximum, minimum and average price guideline of what readers expect to pay for a similar book to yours. Are they higher than your book production costs? If so, great! You now have a baseline from which to move onto the next factor. If not, then you need to go back to the drawing board and reconsider your print specifications to see where you can trim costs.

Factor 3: Value of You

Have you ever noticed that some books on the same subject have a much higher cover price than others and that readers are willing to pay that higher cover price? That is all down to the perceived value of the author and their unique perspective on that topic. So, the next factor that you need to consider when setting an attractive cover price is the unique value that you bring to your readers.

How much experience do you have on the subject that you are writing about? Do you have a unique perspective or are teaching a brand new approach to a common problem? If the answer is yes, then you can start nudging your cover price slightly above the average (but not above the maximum unless you are supremely convinced that you can back it up!). If you're relatively new to the field, then you may need to be realistic and potentially lower the price slightly below the average until you gain more experience and credibility (which publishing your book will do!).

What NOT to factor in: Publishing Investment

A common mistake that I see authors try and do when setting their cover price is to try and factor in their initial publishing investment in an attempt to recuperate their costs as quickly as possible. This is a big no-no and will lead you down the path of figures just not adding up.

Trying to work publishing costs such as editing and book design into your book production costs means that you will need to over-inflate your cover price to come up with a figure that at least resembles a profit. The result of this is that you end up pricing your book out of the market to the point that readers will not buy it. Which when you look at it, puts you in a worse situation than if you kept your publication costs separate.

If you want to read up on my solution to this quandary, check out my recent blog on "5 Powerful Ways to Measure Self-Publishing ROI". It looks at ways that you can account for this initial publication costs and ensure that you do earn that money back... and then some.

Additional Consideration: Wholesale Discount

There is one last consideration that I want to touch on, and that is a Wholesale Discount. It may not have a direct impact on setting an attractive cover price, but it does have an impact on the amount of royalty that you earn as a result of the cover price that you set.

For those of you unfamiliar with the term, a wholesale discount is the discounted price that a retailer (like Amazon or Waterstones) pays for your book for them to sell it to their customer. This is how retailers earn their money.

Some retailers will have a fixed wholesale discount that you have to accept if you want to sell your book in their stores; no ifs ands or buts. If you publish through IngramSpark however, you can determine the wholesale discount that you are willing to offer retailers (within a set range) and the retailer then opts whether to accept your terms and list your book, or not. Again, this is a delicate decision to make – set the percentage too high and you end up giving away most of your profit; set it too low and retailers won't want to list your book (potentially limiting your books' availability).

This is where the IngramSpark Publishers Compensation Calculator (https://myaccount.ingramspark.com/Portal/Tools/PubCompCalculator) that I mentioned earlier comes in handy. In it, not only can you see the effect of different cover prices on your projected royalty, but also different wholesale discounts. This resource is completely free and you don't need to have set up an account with Ingram before you can get access to it, so I strongly recommend that you make good use of it.

So there you have it, the 3 main things that you should consider when setting an attractive cover price for your next self-published book. I hope you have found that useful. If you have, don't forget to subscribe via the link in the side panel so that you can get more great content like this delivered straight to your inbox.

ISBN Numbers: Everything You Need to Know

Many authors I work with find the topic of ISBN numbers quite confusing. So in this article, I'm going to share with you everything you need to know about ISBNs. I'm also going to debunk a few common myths about them.

What is an ISBN Number?

Let's start right at the beginning. ISBN stands for International Standard Book Number and is a unique numeric commercial book identifier. They are used for the ordering, listing, sales and stock tracking of one-off publications worldwide. David Whitaker first developed it in 1967 in the UK. This early configuration was only 9 digits long as it was adapted from the Standard Book Numbering system developed by Gordon Foster, 2 years earlier. In 1970, the ISBN system was adopted by the International Organisation for Standardisation (ISO) and was published as an international standard in a 10-digit format.

In 2006 the ISO anticipated a shortage of ISBNs due to the rapid growth of the publishing industry and in January 2007 introduced the 13-digit ISBN number format.

Each ISBN number is made up of 5 components:

1. EAN Prefix: currently either 978 or 979. This component makes ISBNs compatible with international barcode standards as set by GS1.
2. Registration Group: this component identifies the country, region or territory in which the title was published.

3. Registrant: This identifies the publisher or imprint responsible for the title.
4. Publication: this is the number assigned to the particular edition and format of a specific title.
5. Check Digit: this is a final single digit that is generated from a mathematical equation. It validates the ISBN and helps to prevent fraud.

N.B. Human readable ISBN can be shown with hyphens or spaces

Currently, ISBNs are monitored and controlled by the International ISBN Agency which issues ISBNs to national ISBN agencies for distribution within their region or territory. More about them shortly.

Do I Need an ISBN Number?

If you plan on selling your book through any form of retail channel, then you need to have an ISBN number. Though it is not strictly speaking a "legal" requirement, nearly all bookstores and retail outlets are run using an electronic point-of-sale system of some kind. These systems are reliant on ISBNs and machine-readable barcodes to work. If your book does not have an ISBN, then they will not be able to sell it.

It is also worth noting that most authors will require multiple ISBNs for each book they publish. Because an ISBN number is assigned to each edition of a book, you will need a separate ISBN number for each edition. For example, if you plan on publishing a book as a paperback, an eBook, and a limited-edition hardback, then you will need three separate ISBNs.

Additional benefits of assigning ISBNs include:

- Correct use of ISBNs allows different editions of your book to be clearly differentiated. This ensures that a customer receives the version they requested.
- ISBNs facilitate the compilation and updating of book-trade directories and bibliographic databases. Meaning that information about your book can be easily found by retailers interested in stocking your book.
- The ordering and distribution of books within the book trade are executed by ISBN number. This is the fastest and most efficient system.
- The accumulation of sales data is done by ISBN number. This enables the varying success of different formats and editions to be monitored and compared.
- National lending rights schemes in most countries are based on ISBN.

Where do I get an ISBN number?

Now that we have established that you need at least one ISBN number, where do you go to get them? Firstly, you need to register as a publisher or self-publishing author with the national ISBN agency for your region or territory. The ISBN agency for the UK is Nielsen Book Services (http://www.isbn.nielsenbook.co.uk), and in the United States, it's RR Bowker (http://www.isbn.org/). A full list of every national ISBN agency is available on the International ISBN Agency website (https://www.isbn-international.org/agencies).

Once you have registered as a publisher, you will be assigned a Registrant Code. After that, you will be permitted to purchase ISBNs in singles or batches of either 10, 100, or 1,000. It is advisable to keep a record of your ISBNs and update it regularly with the titles you have assigned to each number to avoid duplications. I also recommend keeping track of which ISBNs you have submitted metadata records for to the ISBN database.

What About ISBN barcodes?

As mentioned previously, one of the purposes of the ISBN format is to power electronic point-of-sale systems. For this to work, your ISBN number needs to be encoded into a machine-readable barcode. That barcode needs to be clearly printed somewhere on the back cover of your book. There are several free online barcode generators available. If you are going to publish your book through Ingram Spark, their cover template service includes the generation and placement of your ISBN barcode. This ensures 100% compatibility with most point-of-sale systems. It also takes the hassle out of making sure your barcode is machine-readable.

Common Myths About ISBN Numbers

Let's set the record straight regarding several common myths I hear about ISBNs.

Myth #1: You need to renew ISBNs regularly.

I have seen several "less reputable" online publishers try this on with unsuspecting authors, this is categorically not true! ISBNs never expire; not even if the publisher who owns them goes out of business. Once you purchase a set of ISBNs, they are valid for life.

Myth #2: An ISBN number is an assertion of copyright.

According to the absolute letter of the law, no, ISBN numbers do not represent ownership of copyright. However, submitting a listing to the international ISBN database does acknowledge the ISBN owner as the publisher of record for that format and edition of that book. This can greatly aid any argument against a breach of copyright case that is brought to court. But remember that ISBNs are assigned to a particular format and edition of a book, and not to the book as a whole. That is governed by Intellectual Property (IP) regulations, which is an entirely different kettle of fish.

Myth #3: ISBNs cannot be assigned to eBooks.

This myth stems more from confusion surrounding ISBNs and eBooks than anything else. Because eBooks are digital content, they have no stock value and do not need to be scanned by a point-of-sale system to be sold. Therefore, they don't technically need an ISBN number assigned to them. When publishing an eBook directly through Amazon (Kindle) they will assign it an internal reference number or ASIN (Amazon Standard Identification Number). However, that ID number is only for use within the Amazon system. This means that no one else will be able to stock your book, or even know that your eBook has been published. So, I highly recommend that you assign an ISBN number to your eBooks as well as print edition books. It allows you to take full advantage of the benefits that the ISBN identification system has to offer.

So, there you have it, everything you need to know about ISBNs. If you have any questions about ISBNs and how they apply to you as an author, please let me know in the comments section below. And don't forget that if you don't want to have to bother with all this stuff at all, my all-inclusive publishing package includes the purchase, registration, and application of ISBNs to your book. Click this link to find out more (https://swatt-books.co.uk/services/publishing-package).

Choosing the Best Self-Publishing Platform for You: Amazon KDP vs IngramSpark

Self-publishing has become an increasingly popular route for writers to get their work out to the world. With the rise of digital publishing, there are now numerous self-publishing platforms available, including Amazon KDP and IngramSpark. In this article, we will compare Amazon KDP and IngramSpark and help you decide which platform is better for your needs.

What is Amazon KDP?

Amazon KDP (Kindle Direct Publishing) is a self-publishing platform that allows authors to publish and sell their books on Amazon's Kindle store. KDP offers a range of tools and services to help authors create and publish their books in both digital and print formats. KDP is free to use and allows authors to earn up to 70% royalty on the sale of their books.

What is IngramSpark?

IngramSpark is a self-publishing platform that allows authors to publish and distribute their books in both digital and print formats. IngramSpark is more geared towards professional publishers and independent bookstores but is open to individual authors as well. IngramSpark charges a fee for its services, but they offer more customization options and wider distribution options than KDP.

Comparing Amazon KDP and IngramSpark

Costs

Amazon KDP is free to use, and there are no upfront costs or fees associated with publishing your book on the platform. Amazon takes a percentage of each sale as their commission, but authors can earn up to 70% royalty on the sale of their books.

IngramSpark charges a fee for their services, including a setup fee and a fee for each print-on-demand book printed. They also take a percentage of each sale as their commission, but authors can earn up to 45% royalty on the sale of their books.

Customization and Formatting

Amazon KDP offers a range of formatting tools to help authors create their books in both digital and print formats. However, the customization options are limited, and authors are restricted to Amazon's formatting requirements. KDP does not offer any support for creating hardcover books.

IngramSpark offers more customization options, allowing authors to create books with their own formatting and design. IngramSpark supports hardcover books, and authors can choose from a wide range of paper and binding options.

Distribution

Amazon KDP offers distribution through the Amazon Kindle store, which is the largest eBook retailer in the world. Amazon also offers print-on-demand services through their subsidiary company, CreateSpace.

IngramSpark offers wider distribution options, including distribution to major online retailers such as Amazon, Barnes & Noble, and Apple Books. IngramSpark also offers distribution to physical bookstores and libraries through its partnership with Ingram Book Group.

Support

Amazon KDP offers basic support through their online help centre, but they do not offer personalized support for individual authors.

IngramSpark offers more comprehensive support, including a dedicated support team and access to Ingram's network of publishing professionals.

Which platform is better?

The answer to this question ultimately depends on your individual needs and goals as an author. Amazon KDP is a great option for authors who are looking to publish and sell their books primarily through Amazon. KDP is free to use, and the platform is easy to navigate. However, the customization options are limited, and the support is basic.

IngramSpark is a better option for authors who are looking for wider distribution options and more customization options. While there are fees associated with using IngramSpark, the platform offers a higher level of support and access to Ingram's network of publishing professionals.

In conclusion, both Amazon KDP and IngramSpark are excellent self-publishing platforms. If you are looking to publish your book primarily on Amazon and want a simple, easy-to-use platform, KDP is a good option. If you want wider distribution options and more control over the customization of your book, IngramSpark is a better choice.

Book Distribution: How to 'Go Wide'

Book distribution is one of the areas that many first-time authors considering self-publishing struggle with. The question of how to get your book into the hands of readers is one that will ultimately make or break how successful your book can be.

What complicates matters is that there are several ways in which self-publishing authors can go about distributing their books.

Book Distribution Options

Self-Fulfilment:
This is where you commission a traditional printer to produce a print run of your books and then you send them to where they need to go.

- **PRO:** the cost to produce each copy is lower than other options
- **CON:** you must order a minimum quantity upfront (usually 200-500) which means there is a considerable upfront cost and risk; you need to store them; you need to manage the logistics of shipping yourself which can be time-consuming

Amazon KDP:
Amazon KDP (formerly CreateSpace) is the method that most people think of when you talk about self-publishing. You upload your book to Amazon, and they manage the distribution of it to their customers.

- **PRO:** no account or listing fees, and the cost to print and deliver books is taken out of the cover price

- **CON:** your book is only available through Amazon[23]

IngramSpark:

IngramSpark (the consumer arm of Lightning Source) is a print-on-demand publishing platform just like Amazon KDP, however as they are owned by the largest book distributor in the world, their distribution network will get your book into nearly 30k book retailers, libraries, and universities around the world.

- **PRO:** global distribution that most retailers (both online and brick & mortar) already deal with regularly
- **CON:** Though your book will be available to purchase on Amazon, Amazon does not consider whether a book is available as print-on-demand or not outside of KDP, so you run the risk of your book being temporarily out of stock – especially during the few first week weeks of publication.

There are many other print-on-demand platforms, but KDP and IngramSpark are the two largest.

As you can see, there are a few big cons to each of the various book distribution methods. But there is a distribution method that is starting to gain momentum in the self-publishing industry, and that is the concept of 'Going Wide'.

'Go Wide'

Going Wide is the approach of combining all three book distribution methods I mentioned above together to make use of all the benefits and offsetting the negatives. Here's how it works:

1. You list your book on Amazon KDP in both print and Kindle. This ensures that your book is available across the Amazon network, and you don't run the risk of it ever being listed as out

of stock as Amazon's algorithm knows that it's a print-on-demand title.
2. You replicate that same listing on IngramSpark in both print and generic eBooks. This then distributes your book to retailers outside of Amazon (like Waterstones, Barnes & Noble, The Book Depository, and Booktopia). You also use IngramSpark to order small quantities of author copies of your book at cost price to fulfil any face-to-face sales, gifts to clients, friends, and family, or for marketing purposes.
3. Then if you should ever need a high volume of books for an event or a big promotion (more than 250 copies) you send the same artwork that you submitted to IngramSpark and KDP to a traditional printer.

By using this method of book distribution, you eliminate the considerable up-front costs and risk of printing a load of books without knowing whether they will sell. You avoid the necessity of shipping books to your readers or negotiating distribution accounts with individual retailers and book distributors like Gardners or Bertrams. Yet you retain control over how your book is made available to the public and your royalties are automatically paid to you each month.

If you want to learn more about how the Wide book distribution model works, check out my book "Stress-Free Self-Publishing" available on [Amazon](#), [Waterstones](#), [Barnes & Noble](#), and all other fine book retailers. Or you can get a [signed copy direct from me](#).

Copyright in Self-Publishing: What You Need to Know

I have long put off writing an article on copyright in self-publishing; mainly because it is not my area of expertise. However, it is an area where I see a lot of authors making mistakes that could potentially be very damaging simply through making assumptions. So, I'm going to give you a high-level overview of the things you need to know about copyright and how it pertains to you as a self-publishing author, and then leave you with a list of resources on where you can find more information.

In this article I'm going to touch on:

- What is copyright
- Copyright overseas
- Copyright duration
- Using copyrighted material
- Protecting your copyright

So, let's get into it.

What is copyright

Copyright is a form of intellectual property protection that is granted to the original creator of a work by law and prevents others from using it without the creator's permission. It is assigned automatically whenever an individual creates a piece of work that is original and exhibited some degree of labour, skill, or judgement in its creation[23].

Copyright protects your book by preventing people from[25]:

- copying your work
- distributing copies of it, whether free of charge or for sale
- renting or lending copies of your work
- performing, showing, or playing your work in public
- making an adaptation of your work
- putting it on the internet

It is worth noting that copyright can be owned by more than one individual and can also be sold or licenced to a third party.

Copyright notice

Even though copyright is granted automatically and does not require any form of prior registration, it is in your best interest as an author to include a copyright notice in your book to deter copyright infringement. This notice simply makes it clear that your work is subject to copyright and provides a means of identifying you as the copyright owner.

I copyright notice does not need to be complicated. It consists of the word 'Copyright', the copyright symbol (©), the year of publication, and the name of the copyright owner. For example:

Copyright © 2021 Samantha Pearce

Copyright ownership

Copyright ownership can get a little complicated, especially when it comes to books, but in most cases, the author of the book is considered the first owner and copyright holder. There are 4 areas where this ownership gets a little murky:

1. Works created for an employer: If you write a book as an employee for a company, the company/employer is considered the first owner.
2. Commissioned works: The exception to the rule is if you were commissioned to write the book by a company and were working under a "contract of services". In this case, the ownership remains

with the freelancer/contractor unless there is a contractual agreement handing the copyright to the company on payment.
3. Joint authors: If two or more people contributed to a single book and the contribution of each author is not distinct from that of the other authors, they all may be considered joint owners of the copyright.
4. Co-written works: If the contributions of each author are distinct or separate (for example each writes a specific chapter), then copyright ownership is assigned to each part.

Moral rights

There is a secondary aspect to copyright that authors should be aware of, and that is Moral Rights. Moral rights are concerned with the protection of your reputation as an author. They exist separately from economic rights and cannot be sold or given away, but they can be waived. Some publishing contracts will request you waive your moral rights, but this is not generally recommended. Two fundamental moral rights belong to the author of a copyrighted work:

- The right to claim authorship.
- The right to object to any treatment or use of the work that would be "prejudicial to personal honour or reputation".

Copyright qualification

Even though copyright protection is granted automatically; because it is under the jurisdiction of national state law, there are a couple of requirements for a work to qualify under UK copyright law. They are either:

- The author is a British citizen/national/subject/protected person, an individual resident in the UK at the time of publication, or a company/organisation incorporated by law in the UK.
- Or first publication of the work took place in the UK.

Each country has its own copyright laws, so it is worth checking with your regional government as to the copyright law is in your country. Some countries have accepted a more international copyright convention; please see the next section on Copyright overseas for more.

Copyright overseas

Even though copyright law is under the jurisdiction of national state law, your work could be protected by copyright in other countries through international agreements such as The Berne Convention.

The Burne Convention was first adopted in 1886 as an agreement to honour the rights of all authors who are nationals of the member countries of the Convention of which there are currently 179 (a full list of convention signatories is maintained by the WIPO).

The Convention sets out that for the period of copyright, the copyright owner has the following exclusive rights[26]:

- The right to authorise translations of the work.
- The exclusive right to reproduce the work, though some provisions are made under national laws which typically allow limited private and educational use without infringement.
- The right to authorise public performances or broadcasts, and the communication of broadcasts and public performances.
- The right to authorise arrangements or other types of adaptation to the work.
- Recitation of the work, (or of a translation of the work).
- The exclusive right to adapt or alter the work.

Although the Convention sets out a copyright duration, this is in fact the minimum period of protection provided by signatory countries. The national laws of individual countries often provide a longer copyright duration. Please see the next section on Copyright duration for more detail on how long that is.

Copyright duration

As mentioned above, the Berne Convention set out a minimum copyright period, which is the life of the author plus 50 years. However, national copyright law stipulates how long copyright lasts in that nation, so the actual duration can vary between nation-states.

In the UK, copyright protection starts as soon as the work is created, but the length of copyright depends on the type of work. For written works such as books, that period is the life of the author plus 70 years from the end of the calendar year in which the author died. Where the work has more than one author, the copyright expires 70 years after the death of the last surviving author.

Expired copyright

Once the term of copyright protection expires, the work falls under a public domain licence. This means that the work in effect becomes public property and may be used freely. Once a work has entered the public domain, no one can claim the copyright back.

Using copyrighted work

By the very definition of copyright, you cannot copy or use copyrighted material without permission. You may only use the work of others if:

- The copyright has expired.
- Your use of the work is fair dealing as defined under the 1988 Copyright Designs and Patents Act (UK) – see below.
- Your use of the work is covered under a licensing scheme that you have subscribed to, and that the copyright holder is a member of.
- The copyright holder has given you permission.

In all the above situations, the creator may still retain their Moral Rights regarding how their work is used.

Fair Dealing

Fair dealing (also referred to as fair usage, free use, or fair practice) is a framework designed to allow for the lawful use or reproduction of work without having to keep permission or infringe on the interests of the copyright owner.

The Copyright, Designs and Patents Act of 1988 outlines three instances where fair dealing is a legitimate defence for using copyrighted work[27]:

- If the use is for the purposes of research or private study.
- If it is used for the purposes of criticism, review, or quotation.
- Where it is utilised for the purposes of reporting current events (this does not apply to photographs).

It's this second instance of quoting other work that particularly relates to authors. The Society of Authors advises that limited citations of a work are allowed if used solely for the purpose of critique or review under the following conditions:

- The work is publicly available.
- The source of the work is acknowledged.
- The quoted material is supplemented by topical discussion or assessment.
- The extent of the material quoted is considered an acceptable amount for the purpose of review.

However, it is worth noting that a statutory definition of what constitutes fair dealing does not exist. If a copyright enforcement claim is made in a fair dealing case, it will always come down to the fact, degree, and interpretation of each case. Factors that have been identified by the courts as relevant in determining whether a particular dealing with a work is fair include[28]:

- does using the work affect the market for the original work? If the use of a work acts as a substitute for it, causing the owner to lose revenue, then it is not likely to be fair.
- is the amount of the work taken reasonable and appropriate? Was it necessary to use the amount that was taken? Usually, only part of a work may be used.

The relative importance of any one factor will vary according to the case in hand and the type of dealing in question.

Protecting your copyright

Copyright protection is automatic under national and international law, however there a few things you can do to further protect your work.

The easiest thing you can do is to ensure that you use a correctly worded copyright notice as part of your book. Though, as mentioned above, a copyright notice is not required to enforce copyright, displaying a notice demonstrates that you have an awareness of copyright and that you take infringement of your work seriously.

Copyright registration

If you are especially concerned about the possibility of your work being used without your permission, you can register your work with a copyright registration service, such as The UK Copyright Service. Registration provides verifiable proof of the date and content of your work but be aware that there are costs involved in registration.

Copyright evidence

It is a good working practice to keep supporting evidence of your work to prove your copyright ownership if someone attempts to copy your work.

Copyright evidence falls into two categories:

1. **Evolution of ideas:** This is evidence of the progression of your work such as early drafts, a synopsis, or rough sketches that prove the work progressed over time as opposed to being copied from somewhere else.
2. **Footprints:** This is normally evidence inserted into a finished document that can identify you as the author, such as deliberate mistakes, hidden dates, or watermarks.

Enforcing your copyright

Unfortunately, no matter how many precautions we take, breaches of copyright (known as 'infringement') do take place. If you are faced with that situation, here are some steps that you can take:

1. Be clear that an infringement has taken place; that it is not a case of incidental inclusion and that it is beyond the realms of fair dealing.
2. Gather your evidence of the infringement which should include as a minimum a copy of the infringing work, a copy of your original work, and your copyright evidence discussed above.
3. Contact the infringing party and request they stop using your work or come to an agreement with them for their continued use (such as a licence).
4. Use mediation if your initial request was ignored or not resolved. The Intellectual Property Office offers a copyright mediation service but be aware that the fees involved in mediation depend on the type and length of the mediation session.
5. Your final recourse is to take legal action. It is a criminal offence to breach copyright, so you can file for legal proceedings through the Intellectual Property Office or the courts. If things progress this far, you may also want to engage an intellectual property professional such as an IP lawyer to help you.

Copyright resources

Finally, here is a list of resources that you can use to get more information. Your first port of call should be government resources, seeing as they are the ones who write copyright law. There are also several copyright licencing services that can help you track down copyright ownership for work that you would like to use in your book and to manage licences from other people wishing to use your content. Finally, there are copyright registration services that can help you to further reinforce your copyright ownership.

Government Resources

UK Government Resource on Patents, Trademarks, Copyright and Designs (https://www.gov.uk/browse/business/intellectual-property)
UK Government Resource on Intellectual Property (https://www.gov.uk/topic/intellectual-property/copyright)
UK Intellectual Property Office (https://www.gov.uk/government/organisations/intellectual-property-office)

Copyright Licencing Services

Copyright Licensing Agency (https://www.cla.co.uk)
Publishers' Licensing Services permissions request tool (https://plsclear.com)
Authors' Licensing and Collection Society (https://www.alcs.co.uk)

Copyright Registration Services

The UK Copyright Service (https://copyrightservice.co.uk)
CopyRight (https://copyright.co.uk)

What You Need to Know About Legal Deposits

Many first-time authors are surprised to learn that Legal Deposit obligations are in fact a requirement that is written into law in many countries… and as a self-publishing author, the responsibility for submitting your Legal Deposit copies falls squarely on your shoulders, as do the consequences for non-compliance. To make sure that you don't fall foul of the law here is a basic primer on what you need to know about Legal Deposits.

What is Legal Deposit & Why Do We Have It?

Legal Deposit is basically the system by which all published works are catalogued and stored in a central location. This ensures that published intellectual works are preserved for future generations and become part of the national heritage. Deposited publications are made available to visitors of the central deposit libraries to view and read on the premises, which allows unprecedented access to rare and out-of-print material. Publications are also recorded in online catalogues creating an essential research resource for future generations.

History of Legal Deposit Within the UK

The Legal Deposit system dates to 1610 when Sir Thomas Bodley obtained a written agreement from the Stationers' Company to permit the library that he rebuilt at the University of Oxford (The Bodleian Library) to claim a copy of everything printed under royal licence. The agreement was then extended in 1662 to include the Royal Library and the library at the

University of Cambridge. In 1709 the concept of the Legal Deposit was enshrined in UK law as part of the Copyright Act signed by Queen Anne.

When the British Museum and its Library were established in 1753, they were also added to the list of Legal Deposit libraries. In 1801, that list was further extended to nine libraries in total; however, this was then reduced back down to five: The British Library, the Bodleian, Cambridge University Library, the National Library of Scotland and Trinity College, Dublin. The National Library of Wales in Aberystwyth was later added to the list in 1911 to comprise the six Legal Deposit libraries that we have today.

How to Comply with Legal Deposit Legislation in the UK

As a self-published author, you must provide one copy of every print publication you produce within one month of its official publication date. This needs to be sent to the Legal Deposit Office at the British Library free of charge. The copy deposited must be "of the same quality as the best copies which, at the time of delivery, have been produced for publication in the United Kingdom" according to the Legal Deposit Libraries Act 2003. You can find details of where to send your initial Legal Deposit copy here.

At the point of publication, this is your only 'legal' requirement. The other five Legal Deposit libraries then have one year from the date of publication to request additional copies – usually issued via the Agency for the Legal Deposit Libraries. If you should receive a request for additional copies, that request then becomes legally binding. You can find details of where to send your additional Legal Deposit copies here.

What You Need to Deposit

The Legal Deposit Libraries Act 2003 applies to the following categories:

- Books (including pamphlets, magazines, or newspapers)
- Sheet music or letterpress
- Public maps, plans, charts, or tables

- New editions of existing publications may contain corrections, amendments, or additional content.

What You DON'T Need to Deposit

You are not required to deposit the following types of works unless a written demand for them is made by a Legal Deposit library:

- Reprints of publications already deposited, where no changes have been made
- Internal reports
- Examination papers
- Local transport timetables
- Appointment diaries
- Wall and desk calendars
- Posters.

What if my publication doesn't have an ISBN?

If your publication does not bare an ISBN (International Standard Book Number) or ISSN (International Standard Serial Number) but it has been published, you are still obligated to submit a Legal Deposit copy.

The requirement to deposit a publication does not depend on it being allocated an ISBN number, but on whether it can be considered published – when copies of it are issued to the public. The place of publication or printing, the nature of the imprint or the size of the distribution of that work is irrelevant. It is the act of making a publication available to the public within the United Kingdom that renders a work liable for Legal Deposit.

What if my publication is in electronic format only?

Electronic publications are also governed by Legal Deposit regulations. If your publication is not available in a printed format for deposit in the above fashion, the British Library has several methods for submission depending on the medium or format of the publication and the number of publications you produce per year. You can find more information about digital Legal Deposit submissions here.

Legal Deposit Outside of the UK

It is worth noting that the Legal Deposit system is not restricted to just the United Kingdom. Most major countries have their own Legal Deposit guidelines and regulations, and legislation can and often does vary from country to country.

For example:

- Canada requires that two copies of each work be deposited within 7 days of publication
- Germany requires that in addition to a copy that is to be deposited with the German National Library, you are also required to submit an additional two copies to the federal repository of the state in which the work was published
- In Hong Kong, the time allowance for Legal Deposits to be made is one month
- Monaco states that if a publication produced fewer than 100 copies you must deposit two copies to the state library, otherwise, 4 copies are required for deposit
- In Portugal, publishers are required to deposit 11 copies of all publications
- In the United States, the Legal Deposit requirement also extends to the US government in which the Government Publishing Office is required to submit copies of all publications to over 1,250 federal depository libraries across the country.

Be sure to research what the Legal Deposit regulations are in your country *before* your book is published to ensure that you can comply with all regulations.

So, there you have it; a birds-eye overview of the Legal Deposit system and how you can be sure that your books and publications remain compliant.

3 Simple Rules for Awesome Book Marketing on Social Media

Book marketing is a subject that a lot of first-time authors that I speak to are worried about. After all, writing and publishing a book is a big investment of both time and money; you want to make sure that you see some level of return on that investment.

Now, I'm not an expert on book marketing per se… for that, I recommend you talk to the lovely Karen Williams at Librotas (https://librotas.com). But I have published two books that both achieved the ROI goals that I set for them quickly after publication, and I've seen what a lot of my successful authors have done to market their books. The key thing that I've learned is that A) book marketing doesn't have to be complicated or expensive, and B) that marketing a book is no different from marketing your business.

As a side note, the return on your investment of publishing a book doesn't just have to be copy sales. To learn more about the various ROI opportunities there are for books, check out my article "5 Powerful Way to Measure Self-Publishing ROI"

In this article, I'm going to take a look specifically and book marketing on social media; simply because it is the easiest to implement, it can be done completely free of any cost, and you can start doing it at any time – you don't need to wait until your book is on sale, and the same rules apply if you want to revitalise a book that has been on sale for a while.

There are 3 simple rules for effective book marketing on social media; regardless of what platform you use:

1. Little and Often

This was a rule I learned the hard way when I published "Stress-Free Self-Publishing" back in May 2019. I made the very common mistake of thinking I had to do everything all at once as soon as the book was officially published, and I ended up burning myself out. The other risk with this tactic is that your readers get bored of seeing your post constantly about your book and they switch off.

The trick is to post little bits about your book as often as you can realistically sustain it over a long period. Effective book marketing is all about playing the long game. Little reminders that you are an author, that you have published a book, and that book could be the solution to someone's problem without being pushy, overwhelming, or overburdening yourself with a posting schedule that you can't maintain.

A great trick to make this a little bit easier – and more effective in the long run – is to think of lots of different ways of talking about your book. Some will be the 'buy my book' type of posts, but as any social media marketer will tell you sales posts should only make up a maximum of 20% of your content. The rest can be things like sharing quotes from your book, re-posting reviews, starting a conversation about a topic you write about in your book, sharing your insider experience of being a writer and your publishing journey, the list can go on and on. The more varied your content, the less likely people will get bored of it, and the easier it will be for you to achieve the goal of posting regularly without overwhelm.

2. Consistency is King

The rule of consistency applies to two aspects of your social media book marketing, and they are: be consistent with when you are posting as well as what you are posting.

Regarding 'when'… take what you learned from rule number 1 and work out what a realistic posting schedule could be for you that you could easily maintain over an extended period. Whether that is once a day, once a week, or once a month, it doesn't matter. What matters is that you stick to that schedule consistently. Sure, life happens sometimes that can throw your schedule off, but a good tip to minimise the impact of these hiccups is to write out a posting schedule and then use any of the various social media management services out there that automate posting for you (such as Buffer, Hootsuite, of my personal favourite CoSchedule).

As for 'what'… aim to maintain a consistent style to your posts in terms of writing style, branding, imagery, etc. as this will make it easier for your audience to recognise your posts and start to build a relationship with them.

3. Be the Solution

This final rule goes a long way towards helping achieve that 20/80 split in the content type that I mentioned under rule number 1.

When you wrote your book, you had a purpose in mind for how your book could help your reader. Your book marketing is where you share that purpose with the world. Make it clear that your book solves a particular problem for your target audience. The key to unlocking the true potential of this rule is altruism. By being willing to give small snippets of your support/knowledge/advice to people without any expectation of return, the more people will build an affinity with you and want to either support you back or want to learn more from you – both quite often lead to people going any buying your book.

So, make actively posting comments on other people's posts part of your book marketing strategy. By offering advice, giving recommendations, and **being** the expert with the solution, you start to convert those whom you help to rave fans who will then go and market you to their followers. When that happens your book marketing starts to grow exponentially and beyond your immediate network. Very powerful stuff!

There you have it; 3 very simple rules that will help you form a social media book marketing strategy that will keep you moving in the right direction of achieving your self-publishing goals.

What Happens to Your Royalties After You Die?

This might seem like a very morbid question, but it is one that I've been asked several times recently. So, I asked for some advice from a colleague of mine who specializes in estate preservation and bloodline planning, and here is what he had to say...

Book royalties can be a significant sum of money over time and may be something that you need to consider when writing your Will. Many writers have seen their books gain in popularity post their death so the first thing you need to make sure of is that your royalties continue to be paid after your passing (probably not what you were thinking when you signed up but worth checking into). Once you know you have continued royalties post-death here are a few things you may wish to consider.

Lasting Power of Attorney

If your royalty payments are currently significant then it is likely that you have already established a limited company where those royalty payments are made to. If you have then the first thing you need to consider is putting in place a Business Lasting Power of Attorney (LPA) so that should you fall ill but not pass away, you have selected the best person you know to manage your royalties until you recover. A business LPA is different from a personal LPA because the people you would select to run your business may be completely different as you are looking for people with Business skills not a personal connection to you.

Very clearly you still must trust these people, but you need to recognize that often your chosen partner is not always fully equipped to run your business and make the decisions needed to ensure when you recover there is still a business to return to. Your partner can, of course, be one of your Attorneys but if they don't have the specific skills, you are looking for you can include others who do.

Will

Having protected your royalties while you are still alive it is a simple case of getting a Business Clause included in your Will so you can make specific decisions about who is to benefit from your business upon your death.

Businesses pass Inherence Tax-free between family members so unless you are looking to pass the business outside the family you will not need to establish a specific trust for the Business. If you are leaving the Business to a non-family member, then you would be wise to get the business passed into a trust so that can benefit from the most advantageous tax position at the time of your passing. Depending on the size of your business and your plans for it on your passing there are a variety of options available.

If your royalties are currently not significant enough for you to have already set up a company to manage them but you still wish to leave them to somebody you can include detailed instructions to your Executors in your Memorandum of Wishes (MoW) (document that sits alongside your Will) as to how they should be handled. It is worth noting that MoW's are primarily designed for Goods and Chattels so your instructions will need to be very clear about how this should be handled.

It is worth considering that although royalty payments may be low today, they could increase over time. So, it may be sensible to look at setting up a company to handle that eventuality and then updating your Will as already described.

Kept Assets Limited are a specialist advisory firm that can provide you with our Will writing or estate planning service.

With a little help from Kept Assets Limited, you can plan your estate to provide for the three main factors that can affect your intended outcomes:

Protection: Ensuring you can enjoy your assets and that they cannot be taken away from you whilst you live, perhaps in the event of divorce or the requirement for long term care.

Direction: Keeping faith with your intentions where you have bequeathed assets, items or money to specific groups, individuals, or charities.

Mitigation: Working within the law to reduce the effect of taxation on your estate assets as they pass down to your beneficiaries and, where applicable, future generations.

Want to know more about our will writing or estate planning service and work with a team that have your interests at heart and will advise you to gain the best possible outcome?

Why not call today on 01635 959111 or email grant@keptassets.co.uk

SAM **PEARCE**

Part 4: ...on Authorpreneurship

Why More Authors are Choosing to Self-Publish

It's no secret that more and more authors, even those who have been traditionally published in the past, are turning to self-publishing. But why? What is all the hype about?

Well, here is my take on the 9 reasons why so many authors are going indie.

1. Higher Royalties

This is the obvious one and the reason you will see bantered around the most. But how much higher is 'higher'?

If you are lucky enough to get a book deal from a traditional publisher, and if you have a very good literary agent who is a star negotiator, you can get an advance of a couple of grand and between 7-10% of each book sold depending on your fan base and the 'clout' you bring to the table. 15-20% royalty is not unheard of; however, those sorts of rates are usually reserved for the JK Rowling's, Steven King's, and James Peterson's of this world.

Compare that with self-publishing where you can expect to earn between 50-70% of your cover price depending on the wholesale discount you offer. This does however require you to do your homework into setting a cover price that covers your production costs, with enough margin built in for both you and the bookseller whilst remaining competitive.

2. Creative Control

This is another popular reason that you will hear a lot.

When you sign a book deal with a traditional publisher you are basically signing over the rights to your book. If during the editing process, the in-house editor that the publisher has hired suggests changes to the book that you don't agree with – tough luck. You can argue your case, but at the end of the day, it is the publishers' call. Same with cover design; the publisher may ask for your input, but as they are footing the bill for the designer, they have the final say. They will always opt for what is going to sell the greatest number of copies, which may not always be what is best for the book.

With self-publishing, yes you pay for the editor and designer out of your pocket, however, it will be a much more collaborative process because YOU are the paying client. Your opinion and what you want matters. Obviously, you want to acknowledge that they are professionals, and you are hiring them for their expertise, but you are more involved in the entire process.

3. Quicker to Market

This is also a common reason to self-publish, but one that is strangely not talked about as often.

The entire process of getting traditionally published takes a long time, and you need to have the patience of a saint! Once you've written your book, you first must find an agent. Then you need to go through the arduous process of pitching to publishers and waiting for the inevitable stream of rejection letters until a publisher finally decides to give you a chance. Only then can the actual editing and production process even start, but you are likely not the only author that the publisher is managing at the time so your book must be slotted into a conveyer belt of other books running through a machine with lots of moving parts where any delay to any book in the chain can have a knock-on effect all the way down the line! Consider yourself lucky if your book sees the light of day within a year.

Contrast that with self-publishing, where you can realistically expect to go from manuscript to on-sale in about 4-5 months. You can condense that timetable down a bit if you are prepared to shop around for editors and designers who can work to your schedule, but make sure you give them enough time to do their job properly.

Being quicker to market is especially beneficial to business authors looking to publish their books in conjunction with an event, as the timescale to put on a professional event like a conference or trade show is about the same time as self-publishing.

4. What You Write Had Value to SOMEONE

This is an aspect of publishing that doesn't get talked about anywhere near as much as it should.

Traditional publishing is a numbers game. Even if you approach a publisher who specialises in books for a particular niche, the first question they are going to ask themselves when evaluating your book proposal is "how many people will buy this book?" If the answer isn't at least five figures, they most likely won't give your book any more consideration. They are in the business of selling books, and generally don't really care about whether your story "needs" to be told.

Because self-publishing has no gatekeepers, if you want to write about collecting pink fluffy unicorns, and you know that there are other people out there who also collect pink fluffy unicorns, then what you have to say has value. The only gatekeeper is you and your ability to reach that ultra-niche of readers. That is why knowing your market and having a marketing plan in place to get in front of them is so important if you are going to self-publish.

5. More Positive Experience

Let's face it; at some point in every author's journey, you are going to be racked with feelings of doubt. The dreaded question "Is my writing good enough?" has woken up even the most successful authors at 2 am somewhere along the way. So why would you want to bombard yourself with more doubt and negativity from the outside world? But that is exactly what you will face when you embark on finding a traditional publisher. You will need to face dozens of rejection letters until you find a publisher willing to give you a shot. Even JK Rowling had the first Harry Potter book rejected 12 times before Bloomsbury signed it for an advance of just £1,500.

However, if you self-publish, the only opinions you need to worry about are the ones that matter most – yours and that of your readers. If you think like a publisher and invest in professional editing, peer review, and the time to do your research, your book will be judged by what you have to say, and not how you say it.

6. Not Tied to a Long-Term Contract

Very few authors take into consideration the length of time that their book will be tied to a traditional publisher when first looking to get a book deal. When you consider how much of your book you are signing away, it's a very important factor to consider. It's not uncommon for publishing contracts to remain in effect for the life of the author plus the term of the copyright (which is 70 years in most territories). That means that your heirs will potentially be tied to that contract too!

With self-publishing, if you purchase the ISBN numbers used in the publishing of your book in your own name, you don't have any of that to worry about. ISBN numbers do not expire and are not transferrable to another publication. So, once you have registered a book against an ISBN number with the governing ISBN agency for your territory, your book is yours to do with as you wish for the term of the copyright. After which you (or your heirs) can request to extend if necessary.

7. Flexibility to Change Anything Anytime

A secret fact about being an author that no one tells you about is that a book is never finished! Even if you are fortunate enough not to discover a typo staring you in the face when you open your freshly printed book for the first time, there are always improvements and changes to be made. Maybe your book hits the bestseller list; or you won a prestigious prize that you want to proudly emblazon on your front cover. Or maybe new information has come to light, or you have changed your opinion of a particular topic in your book that you want to update. If you are tied to a traditional publisher for that book, you must go through all the red tape and argue your case for why the book needs an update. Should you win the battle, and the publisher agrees with you, queue the start of the production process all over again.

On the other hand, if you self-publish that book, you or your designer simply makes the amendments and resubmits the artwork. If the case of a full-on second edition, you just assign a new set of ISBN numbers out of the batch you purchased and repeat the listing process.

8. Biggest Share of Book Market & Growing

It's common knowledge that the self-publishing segment of the book market is growing year on year and has been for the past decade. But what you may not know is that we are reaching a tipping point in the market share of self-published books vs. those published by the "Big 5" publishing houses such as Penguin and Random House. In some market segments, that market share has already tipped in self-publishing's favour. According to the January 2018 report by AuthorEarnings.com, the market share for self-published eBooks in the United States exceeded those from the Big 5 publishing houses by 45.7% vs. 25.6%. Overall sales growth of self-published books also increased more than it did for traditionally published books. Self-published sales figures increased by 2.1% in the last nine months of 2017 compared to the 1.1% sales growth seen in traditional publishing.

9. Leverage to Get a Book Deal

If after reading everything up to this point you will want to get a traditional publishing deal, then work the system in your favour! In recent years, traditional publishers have gotten wise to the potential of self-publishing. Publishing houses now scout the bestseller lists looking for indie authors with the next big thing. When they find it, they can approach the author direct, safe in the knowledge that the book has already proven itself. "Wool", "Fifty Shades of Grey" or "The Martian" ring any bells?

This odd role reversal then puts you firmly in the driver's seat when it comes to negotiating the best terms for your publishing contract. You have something that the publisher wants; just make sure you are smart about what you ask for in return and always, always, ALWAYS have a contracts lawyer review any agreement before you sign on the dotted line.

There is one last point that I want to leave you to consider when you're deciding whether to self-publish or not, and that is this… The average reader doesn't care who the publisher is!!!

If you were to ask a Game of Thrones fan who George RR Martin's publisher is, they most likely wouldn't know. Even I had to look up that it was Harper/Voyager when writing this article, and I've read the series umpteen million times! All the reader really cares about is if the book they are investing time and money to read is worth that investment. Is it well-written? Is it easy to read? Is it entertaining or imparting some level of value of knowledge? That is all that really matters.

Publishing for Entrepreneurs: How a book can help your business & how to write one without losing your mind

I have worked with many different authors over the years, and each of them has varying reasons for wanting to publish their books. Unfortunately, many authors only see a book as a finite object; a goal they want to tick off their bucket list. By doing this, they miss the fact that publishing a book can be a very powerful business tool.

"How?" you ask. Well, beyond getting to add "published author" to your LinkedIn profile, there are 5 key areas where publishing a book can help take your business to the next level.

1. Passive Income.

This is the obvious one and the next most common reason why authors publish. If you are clever about how you publish your book, the price that you sell it for, and back all of that up with great marketing, you can turn a self-published book into an additional revenue stream. Once the initial publishing expenses are out of the way, a book can quietly sit in the background of your business, evening out the inevitable peaks and troughs in your bank account that go hand in hand with starting a small business.

2. Raising Your Profile

This is one of the most powerful advantages of publishing a book to support your business. Subconsciously from a very young age, we are taught to revere books and those who write them. All through our school years, we are instructed to look to books for knowledge and understanding. So, it is no surprise that if you publish a book about your area of expertise, people begin to perceive you as an expert and start to set you apart from others in your field – even those who may have more experience than you.

3. Lead Generation

This is an under-utilised advantage of publishing a book on the same subject that your business is built on. It's the concept of using your book as a sales tool to land bigger clients or contracts. I know of several authors who have made an art of this tactic; giving away copies of their book for free to VIP prospects knowing the advantage it gives them.

Using a book as a sales tool does three things: it gives prospects a low-risk opportunity to try before they buy to see if your concepts/solutions/ideas work for them. It allows the reader to build trust in you, even if they have never met you. Lastly, it provides tangible proof of your knowledge and your ability to deliver it.

4. Expand Your Market

Publishing a book gives you the opportunity to reach a much wider audience than you ever could on your own. No matter how good the systems and processes that you put in place in your business, there are only so many clients that you can serve at any one time. A book allows you to reach a wider range of people and is not restricted by geography or economics. A book also gives you the ability to help people who may not be able to afford your premium products/services, therefore expanding your customer base without the need for additional infrastructure.

5. Marketing Tool

Finally, publishing a book can have knock-on effects on your marketing. It can open the door to getting asked to speak at conferences and events both about your book and your wider business. It also presents the opportunity to set up your own mini-events in the guise of a book launch or a book signing tour around bookstores or events in your field.

I see a lot of people getting scared off of writing a book because of the huge commitment not only of finances but of time and energy. However, when you look beyond a published book as a goal in itself and consider the potential return on investment that a book can have on your wider business, it makes for a very sound business strategy… if you do it properly!

This brings me to the next nugget of information that I want to share with you.

Writing a book can be a very long process, and I see a great many authors (me included) who got stuck at some point along the journey. There are countless reasons why this happens, but generally, they fall into one of two categories: The author didn't know what to do next, or they got easily distracted and knocked off course by other 'things'.

I'm going to share my biggest tip for making the process of writing and publishing a book so much… and that is to **Treat Your Book Like a business!**

If you are reading this blog, you are most likely already an entrepreneur, and as a business owner, you know that the key to starting and growing a successful business is to plan. Writing and publishing a book is no different. By planning out your author journey, you make the process much easier and far less stressful.

Don't worry, a book plan doesn't need to be anything like the big scary financial plans you need to get investors or to keep shareholders happy. It just needs to be a simple one-page business plan that answers 6 fundamental questions: Who, What, Where, Why, How and When.

1. Who

Simply put, who is your book for? Who is your ideal reader? Don't be afraid to really laser focus on this. By narrowing down your ideal reader to a very specific demographic, you're not preventing anyone outside of that demographic from buying your book, reading it, or even enjoying it. You're making sure that the people who you really want to read it, and who will benefit the most from it, are not disappointed. Really knowing who these VIP readers are, allows you to tailor your language, message, and marketing, specifically to them.

2. What

Another easy one – what do you want to share with them? Think about what problem or pain point your reader has and then map out how your knowledge and expertise can help them. The more in-depth you get with answering this question the more useful it becomes as you can use it to start mapping out the structure of your book and plan what your chapters and main headings are going to be. That way, when it comes time to sit down and write, you're simply filling in the blanks.

3. Where

This question starts to touch on the subject of logistics – where do you want your book to be available from, and where will you market it? Using the information you gathered in question 1, you can start to paint a picture of where your ideal reader hangs out, where they shop, and where they get their information. You can then use that to figure out the best publishing route that gets your book into the stores your VIP readers shop in and helps you to formulate a targeted marketing strategy to promote it.

4. Why

This question has two components to it. The first is why will your readers want to read YOUR book? What sets it apart from other books that have been written on the same or similar subject? This is basically your USP. The second component is why YOU want to write this book. It is vitally important to have an answer to this question, preferably one that has a strong personal connection to you. I'm not going to lie, writing a book is hard work. You need a strong personal reason to motivate you when the going gets tough and you find yourself wondering why you are putting yourself through this.

5. How

Again, this is a logistics question, and it covers things like how you will publish. Will you self-publish, or will you try and get a traditional publishing deal? How will you afford it? If you opt to self-publish, there are several expensive services that you will need to outsource and pay for before your book gets to market, and you'll need to know how much those services cost and how you plan on paying for them. This also includes how you will market your book. Will you put some money behind paid advertising, or will you rely on social media and guerrilla marketing tactics?

6. When

This is a very key question that most people completely overlook. If you're like me, you need deadlines to motivate you to get things done. Setting a schedule will help keep you on track and keep the project moving. It is important to tailor the answer to this question around how YOU personally like to work – especially if writing does not come naturally to you. You may find that setting aside small segments of time every day works best for you. Alternatively, if you find it takes you a while to get the creative juices flowing, then you might benefit from carving out large chunks of time from your diary or possibly even taking a writing retreat and dedicating a weekend or a whole week to nothing but writing without distraction. Answering this question also helps you maintain momentum in your marketing leading up to launch. There is nothing worse than talking to a potential reader about your book and having them ask when they can buy it only for you to answer with "I don't know". At least with a rough schedule, you can give them an idea of how long they will need to wait for your book. It also introduces the potential of building up a pre-sales campaign, which can be hugely beneficial to launching your book with a bang.

This may seem like a lot of effort to expend before you've even written a single word of your manuscript but trust me, it is time well spent. Having a good book plan provides clarity, helps you maintain focus, and most importantly helps you overcome the obstacles that will inevitably crop up along your journey to becoming a published author.

Happy writing

Self-Publish or Publisher: Which is Best for You

A debate has raged in the literary community for decades as to whether self-publish or publisher is the best route for authors to take to get their books into the hands of their readers. Both sides of this equation are so evenly matched, it's very difficult to choose a clear winner. There are pros and cons on both sides of the fence, so I feel authors should look at all the facts and make an informed decision as to which publishing route is best for *them* and their book.

We're going to look at seven key aspects of the publishing process and compare how self-publish or publisher match up in each category.

Creative Control

Let's first look at who has creative control during the process of creating your book for public consumption. This involves who has the final say in decisions regarding editing, design, and marketing copy.

Self-Publish	Publisher
• Because you hire the editor, cover artist, and typesetter, you are the client – you have the final say in all creative decisions. • You can make decisions based on what you feel is in the best interest of your readers and your content (considering the professional advice from the author services you hire).	• The publisher uses their own in-house editors, cover artists and typesetters so the project manager in charge of your title makes the final decisions regarding creative. • You may be consulted depending on the individual publisher, but they are not entitled to adhere to your wishes. • Decisions are based on what will sell the most copies, which may not always be what is best for your readers or you as an author.

Deciding Factor: Think about what the purpose of publishing your book is. If it is to simply tell a story, to entertain, or get information into as many hands as possible, then a publisher may be a good option for you. If your content is highly specialised and needs to be portrayed in a particular way to be of the most benefit for your reader, then self-publish is a better option where you will have more control over how that content is presented.

Royalties

The distribution of royalties (or the profit from selling a copy of your book) is wildly different between self-publish and publisher options. The profit of each book is calculated as the cover price, minus any wholesale discount required by the retailer who sells the book, minus production, and distribution costs.

Self-Publish	Publisher
• You keep 100% of the profit from each copy sold. • If you price your book carefully and are economical in setting the print specifications and wholesale discounts for your book, this can range from 40%-60% of your cover price.	• The average publishing contract states a royalty distribution to the author of between 5%-10% of the cover price which is treated as a cost to the publisher. • Many publishers will also incur the additional cost of sales agents whose job it is to sell books wholesale into bookstores that individual authors rarely have the option to do. • The publisher keeps all remaining profit for themselves. • Some publishers include clauses in their contracts that authors only receive royalty distribution once the publisher has recovered all costs of publishing the book.

Deciding Factor: If you are not anticipating selling thousands of copies and you are looking to earn a residual income from publishing, then self-publishing is the more profitable route for you in the long run. However, if you have a large following and are likely to sell in high volumes continually, then going with a publisher may be a better option but be sure to negotiate as much as you can into your initial contract.

Time to market

Next, let's look at the varying amount of time it takes to get a book from raw manuscript to market via self-publish or publisher.

Self-Publish	Publisher
• If you employ all the author services that a publisher would (such as editors, cover artists and typesetters) it can take an average of 3-4 months to go from raw manuscript to having a title on sale.	• Because a publisher is usually publishing several books at any given time, it can take upwards of 12 months from the point a contract is signed to your book being on sale. • This does not include the time it takes pitching your book to agents and publishers to get a publisher to offer you a contract in the first place, and then time to properly negotiate that contract.

Deciding Factor: If you have any sort of deadline of when you want to get your book published, self-publishing is really your only option. This is particularly true if you are publishing a book to support a business, as it is far easier to build a three-to-four-month lead time into your marketing strategy then it is to anticipate what might possibly happen a year from now.

Marketing

This is the one that catches everyone out – who is responsible for marketing a book and its author once it's published?

Self-Publish	Publisher
• Even if you are clever with generating SEO-packed metadata, no one will know your book exists without you telling them – all marketing is down to you as the author. • Good news is that there is an abundance of PR and marketing agencies around that specialise in promoting books and authors.	• As a rule of thumb, publishers will not heavily market your book beyond an initial launch. • Unless the author is well known, or initial sales are very good, publishers will stop any marketing activities once they have recuperated their initial investment. • Any marketing activities the publisher does will usually require involvement or participation by the author (such as book signings and interviews).

Deciding Factor: If you are looking for a free ride when it comes to marketing, I'm afraid you won't find one under either option. The difference between self-publish and publisher here is all down to your comfort level with marketing strategies and/or your available budget to invest in marketing support.

Distribution

Historically, distribution was where the large divide between self-publish and publisher options lay –where you could make your book available for sale and how you got it there.

Self-Publish	Publisher
• Using a PoD (print-on-demand) publishing model such as IngramSpark or Amazon KDP can get your book listing in over 7k online bookstores, general retailers, libraries, and universities worldwide with no involvement from the author beyond listing and artwork supply. • Stocking a book in a physical bookstore requires the author to 'pitch' their book to a buying team at each store or chain, but once an agreement has been reached, fulfilment is done PoD.	• The publisher manages all distribution. • Depending on the size of the publisher, they will have distribution agreements already in place with the major booksellers for both online and in-store. • The larger publishers will also have a team of sales reps who visit independent bookstores to sell your book into those retailers.

Deciding Factor: If your book can comply with a standard set of print specifications (such as a standard-sized paperback on uniform paper stock with no special print finishes) then you can achieve the same level of distribution self-publishing as you can going with a publisher and still retain all the other benefits. However, if your book does not comply with PoD specifications in any way, then a publisher is your best bet of getting the widest distribution possible. A self-published author can distribute a non-standard book themselves, however, it requires a lot of logistics and a great deal of involvement from the author.

Cost

The cost of publishing a book and who pays that cost is the biggest difference when it comes to the question of self-publish or publisher.

Self-Publish	Publisher
• The author pays for all costs involved in publishing a book. • Many authors are now turning to crowdfund options to help cover costs in advance.	• The publisher pays for all costs involved in publishing a book. • Depending on your publishing contract, the publisher may also pay the author an advance or signing bonus.

Deciding Factor: Self-publishing a book to similar quality and professionalism as a publisher is not cheap (£2,000-£4,000), so if costs are a concern, then a publisher is your best option. However, with dedication and perseverance self-publishing can be very lucrative and can potentially pay for itself many times over.

Ownership

The final point I want to discuss is ownership, who owns the final published book once all is said and done.

Self-Publish	Publisher
• The author retains full ownership of all aspects of the published book. • If the author also owns the ISBN numbers used in the publishing of that book, they also retain control over that book in terms of whether it remains on sale.	• The author will retain creative copyright over the content of the book, but the publisher will own the rights to the published book. • Some contracts even sign over copyright for a period of time, with the potential for a buy-back of rights.

Deciding Factor: Writing a book can be a very personal thing. If you want to retain full control and ownership of your work, then self-publishing is your only option.

Conclusion

Hopefully, that has helped to breakdown the differences between the self-publish or publisher options when it comes to how you get your book into the hands of your readers.

As you can see, there is no clear-cut right or wrong answer when it comes to which option is best. It's more a question of which option is best for you, your book and what you ultimately want to achieve out of publishing it.

Self-Publishing Triumph: 5 Books That Prove You Can Make It on Your Own

Self-publishing has become a popular avenue for aspiring authors to get their work out into the world without having to go through the traditional publishing route. In recent years, self-publishing has gained immense popularity, and many authors have achieved great success through self-publishing. In this article, we will look at five popular books that were originally self-published.

The Martian by Andy Weir

The Martian is a science fiction novel by Andy Weir, which was first self-published in 2011. The book tells the story of an astronaut, Mark Watney, who is stranded on Mars after his crewmates leave him behind, thinking he's dead. Watney is forced to survive on the planet using his wit, intelligence, and the resources at his disposal. The book became an instant hit and gained a large following, leading to it being traditionally published in 2014. The book was later adapted into a successful movie starring Matt Damon.

Eragon by Christopher Paolini

Eragon is a young adult fantasy novel by Christopher Paolini, which was self-published by Paolini and his parents in 2002. The book follows the story of a young farm boy named Eragon, who discovers a dragon egg and becomes embroiled in a war between good and evil. The book was a huge success, and it caught the attention of publishing giant Random House, who later republished the book in 2003. The book went on to become a New York Times bestseller and spawning several movie adaptations.

Fifty Shades of Grey by E.L. James

Fifty Shades of Grey is a romance novel by E.L. James, which was originally self-published as an eBook in 2011. The book tells the story of a college student, Anastasia Steele, who enters a BDSM relationship with a wealthy businessman, Christian Grey. The book became an instant success, and it quickly gained a large following, leading to a traditional publishing deal with Vintage Books. The book went on to become a global sensation, selling over 150 million copies worldwide and sparking an immensely successful movie trilogy.

Still Alice by Lisa Genova

Still Alice is a novel by Lisa Genova, which was self-published in 2007. The book tells the story of Alice Howland, a linguistics professor who is diagnosed with early-onset Alzheimer's disease. The book gained critical acclaim and caught the attention of traditional publishers, leading to a publishing deal with Simon & Schuster in 2009. The book went on to become a New York Times bestseller and was adapted into a successful movie starring Julianne Moore.

The Joy of Cooking by Irma S. Rombauer

The Joy of Cooking is a classic cookbook by Irma S. Rombauer, which was self-published in 1931. The book contains a comprehensive collection of recipes and cooking techniques, and it quickly gained a following among home cooks. The book's success caught the attention of the publishing company Bobbs-Merrill, who later republished the book in 1936. The book has since been reprinted numerous times, with over 18 million copies sold worldwide.

Self-publishing has become a popular avenue for authors to get their work out into the world, and these five books serve as a testament to the success that can be achieved through self-publishing. These books have all gone on to achieve incredible success, both critically and commercially, and they continue to inspire aspiring authors to take their writing careers into their own hands.

5 Powerful Ways to Measure Self-Publishing ROI

Self-publishing ROI (Return on Investment) can be a touchy subject in the world of self-publishing. Since I became involved in self-publishing in 2015, I've spoken with numerous authors about their motivations for wanting to publish their books. I have heard a myriad of reasons as wide-ranging and varied as the subjects those authors have written about. But no matter your motivations for writing; self-publishing is a considerable investment and at some point, you will want to see some sort of return on that investment.

Many authors become blinkered by the idea that the only way to measure the ROI of your self-publishing investment is through copy sales. And yes, that is certainly the easiest way; but it is by no means the only way.

Here are my 5 top ways to measure self-publishing ROI, so that you can truly judge whether you and your book have achieved what you set out to do by publishing it.

1. Book Sales

Book sales are the gold standard of measuring self-publishing ROI, as it's the simplest equation. Money spent minus money earned equals ROI. As soon as the resulting figure equals zero, you've recuperated your investment.

The best way to track this is to calculate your break-even point in terms of the number of copies you need to sell to recuperate your initial publishing investment. During the book listing process, whether you are using Amazon KDP or IngramSpark, you will be told how much profit (royalty) you will earn from each copy sold through a retail channel. Take the total financial investment you have spent to publish your book (excluding any PoD printing costs) and divide it by the royalty amount. That is the number of books you need to sell to recuperate your investment.

If you are not publishing via a Print on Demand (PoD) service and are selling your books via a self-fulfilment model using a Fulfilled by Amazon (FBA) account, then you do need to add the cost of getting each batch of books produced by your printer to your total investment figure. Be sure to include any delivery charges both to you and to your local Amazon distribution centre.

2. New Clients

If you are publishing a book to support your business, then the next best way to measure self-publishing ROI is by calculating it against the financial return of winning a new client because of publishing the book.

Publishing a book on the same subject on which you base your business and then working it into your sales process is a great way to boost your sales almost overnight. The marketing that you put into your book has the dual effect of also marketing both you and your business. In turn, your book will help attract new prospects to you whom you may not have reached with your previous marketing efforts. Also, the quality of those new prospects will be of a much higher calibre as they will come to you already pre-sold both on your business and you as a person with whom they want to work. This all makes the sales process that much easier.

So how do you calculate your ROI based on new client acquisition? Very similar to book sales. Take the average cost of your product/service that you charge to a client and plug that into the book sales break-even equation that we discussed above in place of royalty. So, the equation now reads as total financial investment divided by average product/service cost equals the number of new clients you need to acquire to break even. Unless you are selling a low-ticket price product or service, you will find that this dramatically reduces the number of transactions needed for you to break even!

3. 'Expert' Status

Now we start to get into the less tangible aspects of ROI, in terms of looking at the effect that publishing your book has on you and your surrounding business.

If you've read some of my previous blog posts, you'll know that publishing a book on the same subject on which you base your business helps establish you as the go-to expert on that subject. A natural by-product of being regarded as an expert in a particular field is that people are generally willing to pay more to work with 'the best'.

Though this isn't itself a measurable return on investment, it does have a considerable effect on the New Clients' ROI calculation. If the average cost of your product/service increases by 10%, the resulting number of transactions needed for you to break even reduces by the same amount. Think about what's better… to sell 100 widgets at £10 or 10 widgets at £100?

By the way… this can apply to fiction authors too. Would you consider Stephen King, J.K Rowling or Andy Weir expert writers in their respective genres? Of course, you would. Though this may not mean you can increase the cover price of your books by the same percentages as I mention in client services being offered by non-fiction writers, it can have an impact on the number of books you sell.

4. Speaking Gigs

Another by-product of being regarded as an expert is that people want to know what you know. They want to hear what you have to say and see if they can learn some of your secrets to success. Welcome to the world of public speaking!

This is not for everyone. I know many authors who are amazingly eloquent with a pen but put them on a stage in a room full of real live people and they get tongue-tied over the simplest sentence. If you can master your nerves, start doing speaking engagements at libraries, conferences, and literary festivals. The more you get known on the speaking circuit, the more speaking gigs you get booked for, and soon enough people will start paying you to speak on their stages! This does take time, practice, and patience. But when it all starts to come together, it's yet another source of revenue that you can add to your income pot that helps get you closer to that magical break-even point.

5. Social Philanthropy

Though we live in a very cash-driven society, not all ROI needs to be calculated in pounds and pence, dollars and cents. I know many authors whose only driver for publishing a book is to give back to the community in some form or another. For them, the reward of being able to genuinely help someone is worth the investment of publishing a book.

There is no financial calculation for this type of ROI; it's what you feel is a suitable exchange of investment versus reward. If you can pay your bills, put food on the table, a roof over your head, then giving back to the community through publishing is a noble and honourable pursuit.

As an aside, if this is something that you would like to do, but aren't too sure how to set up, talk to the guys at Work For Good (https://workforgood.co.uk). They make it easy for small business owners and authors to donate to charity through sales by helping to manage all the logistics and legal compliance.

So, as you can see, just as there is more than one way to skin a cat, there are more ways to measure self-publishing ROI than just tracking book sales. By keeping an eye on that all-important break-even number, you will not only feel less stressed about investing in publishing your book, but you will ultimately achieve greater success as a result.

There is a quote that constantly gets circulated in business circles that has been attributed to numerous people in different guises that basically says, "What gets measured gets managed". This is so very true. If you know the target that you are aiming for (your break-even figure), and you measure regularly where you are concerning that target, then it is always front of mind what you need to do to reach that target.

So, work out what your break-even figure is, then each month when you receive your sales reports from Ingram or KDP, take a look at how much closer you are. You will be surprised at the impact it can have on your motivation to continue marketing your book… which is a topic for another day.

5 Ways a Book Can Boost Your Credibility

It's no secret that if used correctly, writing, and publishing a book can be a very powerful marketing tool to boost your credibility; not only for your company but also for you as an author and entrepreneur. In this article, I'm going to share with you 5 different ways you can use a book to boost your credibility and how the more you use a book in this way, the more the effect on your credibility starts to compound.

1. Expert status

The first way you can use a book to boost your credibility is as the symbol of your status as an expert in your field.

It is a perception that is ingrained in us from a very young age, that if you want a credible source of information you turn to books. All the way through school, college, university, and professional accreditation courses, you conduct your research using books because we assume that the authors of those books are the experts. There is a reason why the phrase "they wrote the book on it" exists when referring to someone with a high level of expertise.

So simply through the act of writing and publishing a book, you are boosting your credibility by positioning yourself as an expert authority on your subject.

2. Speaking engagements

The second way you can use a book to boost your credibility is as a tool to get public speaking engagements.

As a result of your expert status, people naturally want to know what you know and another way for you to share the knowledge you convey in your book is to talk about it. This can take the form of keynote talks at conferences and events, guest lectures at schools, colleges and universities, workshops hosted either by other industry experts or put on by you, and even readings at book signings and other public appearances.

This starts to compound your expert status from point one, and your name starts to get known in wider and wider circles, boosting your credibility further.

3. Visibility

The third way you can use a book to boost your credibility is through the very nature of marketing itself; getting your name in front of more and more people.

Every piece of marketing you do to promote your book adds to your visibility online and increases the likelihood of someone hearing about you. So, the more you leverage the tactics from points one and two, the more it contributes to your overall visibility. People start to hear/read your name in more and more places which leads them to believe that you must know what you're talking about or why else would so many people be talking about you. This, in turn, piques their curiosity about what all the fuss is about and often they will actively seek out more information about you.

Of course, this can sometimes be a double-edged sword in that people often talk more about the bad than the good. But if you are proactive in maintaining a positive public image it's unlikely that you will be the subject of too much negative press.

4. PR

This leads me to the fourth way that a book can help boost your credibility and that is as a tool in securing PR opportunities.

Members of the press are always on the lookout for credible sources to add weight to their stories in newspapers, magazines, and blogs. Radio, TV, and podcast hosts are always on the hunt for new content and guests to keep their audiences entertained and informed. The increased visibility that you get because of leveraging the first three points puts you top of the list to fill these PR opportunities.

People will either start to approach you for interviews, give talks/lectures at their events, collaborations, and sponsorships or when you approach others for such opportunities your name will have more weight behind it because of the credibility that you have already amassed from your book marketing activities.

You also have the bonus of having a vault of content from your book to draw on to feed to these journalists, podcasters, and bloggers, which makes things easier for both you and them – win/win.

5. Higher profile client acquisition

The results of all the other four points then combine to enable the fifth and final way a book can boost your credibility and that is as a vehicle for attracting a higher calibre of client who wants to work with you.

Your credibility is often tied to the credibility of those whom you have worked with previously. We see it time and time again in the reaction from people when they see a well-known blue-chip corporation on someone's CV; it tends to stand head and shoulders above the others in the pile.

The boost to your credibility that you have gained from the previous four points all act in concert to put your name in front of those higher-profile clients you dream of working with. It also works to alleviate any doubt they may have had in working with you as you have clearly proven that you know your stuff (or else you wouldn't have built the reputation that you have). This then starts a chain reaction… by adding a high-profile client to your (or your company's) CV, that in turn attracts more high-profile clients, and so on.

The Snowball Effect

As you can see, each of the 5 ways you can use a book to boost your credibility adds to the next. This continues the more tactics you use to promote and use your book as a marketing tool; building more and more momentum as you go.

The great thing is that this process can be cyclical, meaning that the more you repeat it (either for new books you publish or even as an additional marketing campaign to reinvigorate an already published book) the more it starts to snowball. Your credibility as an expert author and speaker in your field of work grows with each application of the process.

Authenticity: how to be genuine when you speak as an author

One of the most effective ways for an author to market themselves and their books is through public speaking. The catch is that many authors are natural introverts; they prefer to write as opposed to present, which makes capitalising on the benefits of public speaking very difficult.

As this is such a common stumbling block for many authors, I have asked international speaking coach Deon Newbronner from Truth.Works to give you some insight and advice on how to be authentic as a presenter.

You have the power to choose what your audience sees in you when you present.

Critical to your success as a presenter is recognising that your audience will be judging you from the moment you go live. They cannot help it and they do not consciously know they are doing it but judging you they are.

An obvious question might be "What judgements are they making?" We judge others based on their observable behaviours. Your audience are judging you based on what they see you do.

Much like your book. Don't we judge a book by its cover?

As a presenter, your behaviours are driven by your values – those things you hold as being important; your ego and wider personality; and your beliefs, fears, and aspirations. It's a complex mix.

In my work with authors all over the world who want to improve their impact and influence on the audiences they present to, many ask how I can be genuine when I must toe a certain line. When I am expected to be a certain way? My first piece of advice, and often the most important and impactful, is to be authentic when you present.

Authenticity is about being genuine and, in the context of presenting, it is about being a version of yourself that is connected to your book when you present rather than being something you think you're not.

What is it to be authentic as a presenter?

If you focus on trying to manage the impression an audience has of you when you present, you are more likely to come across as insincere. It is important to recognise that being yourself when you present might require work on building your confidence in that situation, but confidence is a necessary state to be in if you are to be seen by the audience as both positively impactful and authentic.

The word authentic comes from the Greek word 'authentikos' which means 'genuine'. When you present, it is important to know what you stand for. Your book has a message. You have spent months choosing the right words. Your book says something about who you are. So, when you present your belief and knowledge must come through in your words and actions.

How do I be authentic as a presenter?

As no change is possible without first having self-awareness, a useful thing to do is to reflect on what it is that you stand for as an individual (including your values), as an author and as a presenter. Having considered these things consciously, ask yourself these two specific questions:

- Does the way that I present communicate the things that I believe and feel and that I want others to feel?
- What do I need to do if it does not?

These questions provide a link between knowing what you stand for (what is 'authentic' for you) and how you can demonstrate authenticity.

A lot of research has been carried out into what influences audiences positively, how to make an impactful start, how to structure information to engage and how to maximise the chance of an audience taking action through a strong finish.

All of these techniques and approaches are absolutely aligned with you being authentic as long as what you are presenting and asking of an audience is in keeping with your strongly held beliefs and values. Your core message. If this alignment is in place, then it is much more likely that any approaches you utilise will be effective. Building your confidence as an authentic presenter.

Five practical steps to be authentic as a presenter

Here are my 5 steps to building your confidence in being an authentic presenter:

1. Our values drive our behaviours, thinking and feeling. Work out what these are. Know them, link them to your book's key messages, and use them as your anchor when presenting.
2. Set an intent – a clear motivating reason (for yourself) for presenting. Hold true to this throughout your presentation. The intent you choose must be one of your values, relevant to the presentation, your book, and the audience.
3. Be very clear on your desired outcome and call to action: what, specifically, do you want the audience to know or do because of your presentation?
4. Manage your state to be as confident as possible: be aware of how you feel before a presentation and take steps to build your situational confidence. Some of this can be done in advance through effective preparation and mental rehearsal. In other words, Pause, Breathe and Observe.

5. Take time to structure the content to ensure the audience has all of the key information presented clearly. Not doing this will be an interference for them.

In summary, all presenters can be seen as being authentic when they present. Often, success is down to how much self-awareness you have about what you stand for and how your audience might be perceiving you. This is so that you can be flexible enough with your behaviours to proactively manage their perceptions until this all becomes completely natural and unconscious.

It is important to recognise that all presenters are improving, provided they focus on raising their self-awareness. By focusing on the issue of authenticity you are getting to the very heart of what it is to be a great presenter.

You have chosen what your audience reads about you in your book. You are also choosing what your audience sees in you when you present.

Truth.Works. online Compelling Speaker course will help you be authentic as a presenter. ENROL NOW!

Can You Make Money from Self-Publishing?

Can you make money from self-publishing? It's a question I hear a lot, especially from authors just starting out on their writing journey. It's also the primary battle cry of those who are opposed to the idea of self-publishing as a viable route to becoming a published author. So, let's explore the idea of making money from a self-published book using my own personal experience as a case study.

Since I published my book *Stress-Free Self-Publishing: How to publish your own book without losing the will to live* in May 2019, many people have asked me, "How many copies have you sold?" This is generally the measure of success that most people understand, and a target that most authors set for themselves. It's a concrete figure that is non-arbitrary and can be used to compare the relative success of books across a wide range of subjects and genres. It's also a simple equation to work with when looking at making money: *# of copies sold x £ sold for – printing, shipping & retailer discount = profit.*

The problem lies in the inescapable fact that as a first-time author, it takes a lot of hard work and a generous dollop of good luck to sell a self-published book in large quantities. You're fighting against the fact that no one knows who you are yet and are more than likely publishing a book of which there are already dozens if not hundreds already written on the same subject.

The good news is that the number of copies sold isn't the only measure of publishing success, nor was it a particularly important metric for me.

As a self-publishing consultant, I understand the power that self-publishing a book can have on raising the credibility of an author. So, for me, publishing my book was about establishing my credibility and raising my profile within the author community. It was also about building awareness that there are people like me available to help budding indie authors to self-publish professionally, credibly, and ethically. But how do you measure such abstract concepts against the cost of publishing a book; where does the money come from?

Let's look at some quantifiable figures first. If I paid myself my standard rate to design, typeset and publish my book then *Stress-Free Self-Publishing* cost me £3,800 to publish in both paperback and eBook. This includes the services of a professional editor and cover artist. I invested a further £1,000 in my initial book launch which consisted of marketing materials, a paid and organic social media campaign, and organising a tour of networking events to launch the book to my core demographic of business owners.

During my four-week launch period, I sold 160 copies, which generated a return of £1,140. This meant that my launch campaign paid for itself. A great start, but what about my initial £3k investment to get the book published in the first place?

At the time that I released my book for distribution, I was working on five client books. By the time my launch campaign finished four weeks later, I had 16 client contracts either signed or underway. That 300% growth worked out at roughly £29,000 in additional profit! Sure, some of those contracts would have been signed regardless of whether I published my book or not. However, a high proportion of them can be traced back to two factors.

Firstly, the increased marketing I created surrounding the book launch raised my profile exponentially. Marketing experts say that it takes around 7-10 'touches' for your message to register on a person. That means someone needs to see or hear about you 7 to 10 times before your existence even registers with them for you to then start building the know, like and trust factor required for them to feel comfortable enough to buy from you. People were seeing my name and my book on social media, they were hearing me on the radio, and people were talking about me and my book to their networks who were then talking about it to their networks, and so on. The increase in activity makes it easier and quicker to reach that 7-10 touch points.

Secondly, the content of the book raised awareness of the self-publishing services that I offer to authors. People don't know what they don't know. It's very easy to lose sight of the fact that what seems to be common knowledge to you as an expert in your field, is most likely completely unknown to someone without the benefit of your experience and knowledge. By sharing knowledge and content through not only books but other forms of media, you establish yourself as the source of credible information which in turn builds more trust. The more people trust you, the more likely they are to buy from you. See where I'm going with this?

So, the long and short of it is that self-publishing my book generated a return on investment of £26,000 within just four weeks of its publication when looked at through the lens of new clients and contracts that I won because of publishing and marketing that book.

Now you may be thinking "That's great for those 4 weeks that you're launching a book, but I can't publish a book every couple of months just to keep up that momentum"! The great thing about publishing is that it can have sustainable, long-term benefits for both you and your business long after the book has been published.

My launch campaign for *Stress-Free Self-Publishing* finished at the end of June, which also happens to be my fiscal year-end. The following financial year saw my business achieve 87% growth in income over the previous 12 months. 18 months after publication, that "spike" of new client contracts at the end of my launch campaign has become the new norm. I regularly have between 10-20 book projects live at any given time depending on the season. All it takes is a steady and consistent marketing strategy to maintain that new level. Nothing close to the marketing campaign I did during my launch or else people would get turned off, but just enough to subtly remind them that I have published a book on this subject and that I know what I'm talking about.

And that is where the real magic of self-publishing to support a business lies… in the increase in credibility, profile, reach and expert status that comes from publishing a professional quality book. It *is* possible to measure this impact, but not as quantifiably as profits. For example, because of my increased social media presence, both during my book launch and ongoing, I am being tagged on a regular basis in posts asking for publishing advice in Facebook groups – many from people I've never even met. This is proof that publishing a book about self-publishing has positioned me as the go-to expert on the topic. I am also being invited to speak at a variety of events, as well as being presented with opportunities to share my experiences and knowledge in articles and interviews. Most of which will convert into paying business in the future.

Publishing a book is seen by many experts as the perfect platform for promoting expertise and cementing credibility, just look at the successes of Robert Kiyosaki (*Rich Dad, Poor Dad*), Daniel Priestley (*The Entrepreneur Revolution*, *Oversubscribed*, and *Key Person of Influence*) and Richard Bolles (*What Color is Your Parachute?*). All of which were self-published at some stage.

Some people may assume that my experiences with my book are because of insider knowledge of the self-publishing industry. That my position as a self-publishing consultant affords me access to tips and tricks not available to the average self-publishing author. However, I have seen similar and, in many cases, even more astounding results from other self-published authors.

Still not convinced? Check out these entrepreneur authors who have gone on record to state their author earnings:

- **Renda Derkson,** the Canadian food blogger behind Bewitchin' Kitchen, earns $3k CAD per month as a result of her self-published cookbook based on her favourite recipes from her blog.
- **Michal Stawicki,** the author of the How to Change Your Life in 10 Minutes a Day series, publishes monthly income reports on his blog and earned an average of $3,150 USD per month over the past five months (40-50% of which are book royalties).

- **Alyssa Padgett,** an RV living blogger, is reported to earn about $200 USD a day after self-publishing her book A Beginner's Guide to Living in an RV: Everything I Wish I Knew Before Full-Time RVing Across America.
- **Joanna Penn,** an indie author, and fellow publishing consultant, reported an annual book sales income of $95k USD in 2016 which has only grown in line with the increase in her platform.
- **Pat Flynn,** entrepreneur, and founder of Smart Passive Income, stated in a blog post that he earned $459k USD in direct and indirect income from his book Will It Fly? over a three-year period.
- **Melyssa Griffin,** a business blogger and prolific self-published author, reports monthly earnings of $200k-$300k USD.
- **Timothy Sykes,** a business & investment blogger, and author of An American Hedge Fund is reported to have earned between $15-$20 million USD in a single year according to an article in Forbes magazine.

Self-publishing is not for everyone; it involves dedication, hard work, vision, and planning. But if it looks like it might be for you and you approach the process in the right way – i.e., invest in the professional production and publication of your book, and integrate your book as a marketing tool for your wider business – then YES, you *can* earn money from self-publishing.

Self-Publishing: When to Scrimp and When to Spend

The rise of online book retailers and Print on Demand Technology has turned the book publishing world on its head and transformed self-publishing into a commercially viable option. Despite this, the cost of self-publishing is still significant. My aim in this article is to show you how to spend your money wisely so that you can publish a book that you are proud of and that sells, without breaking the bank.

DIY or Done for You?

It is technically possible to self-publish without engaging any professional support, but I would counsel you to think long and hard before going down this route. Writing your manuscript is only the first in a long line of steps that must be completed if your book has any chance of being successful. And many of these steps require either specialist skills or lots of time and patience.

For example, do you have the editing, proofreading, typesetting, and cover design skills needed? Do you have access to the appropriate design and typesetting software to create a file that is compatible with a commercial printer? Do you have the time to do all of this?

So, what's the solution?

Look for a self-publishing partner who can trust to do as much or as little of the specialist legwork as you need. There are lots of people out there, and standards vary enormously, so make sure that you do your homework carefully before committing your precious cash.

- **Do they have a book publishing track record?** Ask to see samples of books they have been involved with before making your decision.
- **What do their customers say about them?** Ask for references and make sure you follow up with them before making a choice.
- **What's included and what isn't?** Ask for a detailed list of what they will do for you and check for any omissions or hidden extras e.g. Can they handle the conversion of your manuscript to eBook format and if so, is there an additional charge?
- **Bespoke or One Size Fits All?** A bespoke service means you only pay for the services you need.

The benefits of a blended approach

If you are looking to self-publish on a budget, I usually recommend a blended approach where you do the bits you can, while outsourcing what you can't to a professional. Choosing a selective outsourcing approach will usually save you money while ensuring that you maintain control of your book. Let's look at each of the various self-publishing stages to discover the places where you can save money without compromising the quality of the finished product.

Editing and Proofreading

Many authors are reluctant to seek the services of a professional editor only to discover later that their book could have been so much better had they invested in it at this stage.

There are several levels of editing to think about:

- Developmental editing - helps you to get the organisation and structure of your book right.

- Substantive editing - ensures that your manuscript is clear, accurate and readable.
- Copy Editing - checks spelling, grammar, and style consistency.
- Proofreading - a final check that your document does not contain typos and meets typesetting specifications.

Scrimpers tip:

While I recommend that you engage a professional editor/proofreader for the final editing as a minimum, you can keep their costs down by doing the initial editing yourself. In fact, I would recommend that you get as many people as possible to read through and comment on your manuscript, particularly around structure, and readability.

Make sure you choose a wide cross-selection of beta readers you trust for this purpose. Make sure that you include people who are representative of your target readership as well as others who are good at spotting typos and mistakes.

Crowdsourcing such help isn't as difficult as you might think. Tap into the power of your network and ask. Not only does this save you money but it also helps to market your book. Another place to find people to beta test your book is via Goodreads. If you haven't already done so, sign up as a member and then look for the Beta Reader Group.

Book Cover Design

There's an old saying that goes "Don't judge a book by its cover", but when it comes to selling books, the cover design is incredibly important. That's why I would always recommend that you pay for the services of a professional designer with book cover design experience. There's a lot more to designing a good book cover than meets the eye, which is why it is the most outsourced part of the self-publishing process.

Scrimpers tip:

Getting a professional to design your book is a wise investment, but there are ways to keep the costs manageable. For example:

1. The price of stock images can vary enormously, but there are an increasing number of companies selling high-quality, copyright-free, images at low prices. Ask your designer to limit their suggestions to low-cost image options such as Shutterstock. But remember that stock images come with a usage licence that usually limits the number of books they can be used on, so keep in mind potential print runs.
2. Explore the possibilities of bartering. If you have a marketable skill, it often pays to offer an exchange with your designer. Don't assume they will say no, ask!
3. Consider using one of the more reputable freelance bidding sites to find a designer who is happy to work at a lower rate, such as PPH or 99 Designs. I have seen some fantastic covers created by designers in overseas markets such as India and China. Just be conscious of any language or cultural aspects of your cover that could be open to misinterpretation, and make sure that you are VERY clear in your brief as to what you need regarding final artwork specifications.

Formatting for Print and Digital

Print Formatting: Traditionally known as typesetting, book formatting covers a range of skills including font selection, layout design, image sizing and heading and subheading structuring. Get this step wrong, and it could affect the feel and readability of your book which in turn can have a significant impact on sales.

eBook Conversion: Transforming a print manuscript into one or more eBook formats involves an additional set of specialist skills to ensure that your book remains readable despite the different eBook reader screens and font sizes. Unless you have a strong grasp of HTML (Hypertext Markup Language) and understand the code requirements that make the various functions of eReaders work, I would recommend that you have this done by a professional.

Scrimpers tip:

My advice would always be to seek professional help with the formatting of your book as it requires a specialised skill set that most authors don't possess. I have worked with some authors who regretted spending hours formatting their own manuscripts only to find that they looked terrible when printed.

That said, there are things that you can do to keep your costs under control:

1) Agree on the ground rules with your designer up front, especially for things such as layout and font selection. Ask for a sample of text in two or three alternative fonts and layouts so that you can see how it looks before you authorise them to format the whole file. A good designer will then take your chosen sample and turn it into a Master Template which will make typesetting the rest of the book quicker, and therefore cheaper.

2) Colour printing is more expensive than black and white so, unless your book requires colour graphics to be understandable, consider restricting full-colour printing to just your book cover.

3) The size of your book will have an impact on the printing costs, regardless of whether you are printing using traditional Litho methods or using Print on Demand. If you are printing Litho, talk to your printer and ask them to recommend print sizes with less trim wastage as these will use less paper and therefore be cheaper. If you are opting for Print on Demand, take a look at IngramSpark's Print and Ship calculator. It allows you to select different sizes and see how each affects the cost of your book.

Obtaining an ISBN Number

An ISBN number is an international product identifier used by all publishers, and booksellers when ordering and selling books. It is also a legal requirement if you plan on selling your book through an official retail channel. ISBN numbers should be bought via an international book number agency. Nielsen is the ISBN agency for the UK and Ireland. You can buy ISBN numbers singly or in blocks.

Scrimpers tip:

It's MUCH cheaper to buy your ISBN numbers in a block. A single ISBN number currently costs £89 whereas a block of 10 costs just £149. Given that you almost certainly need at least two ISBN numbers per book (one for the print edition and one for the eBook version) you are already saving £29 on your first book, and you still have enough ISBN numbers for your next four books!

Distribution

Surprisingly, it costs little to get your book listed with various online retailers such as Amazon or Barnes and Noble, but it can be time-consuming if you are going to do each one individually.

Scrimpers tip:

I would recommend going with Ingram Spark as it gives your book access to all the main Amazon sites worldwide plus over seven thousand book retailers including Waterstones, Barnes and Noble, and Chapters/Indigo. It's free to register a self-publishing account with Ingram Spark, but there is a one-off set-up fee of $49 per book which includes both a print and eBook edition.

Listing your Book

Before you finally launch your book, it pays to have gathered certain essential information ahead of time. This includes Title, Description, Author Details, Genres, Categories, Keywords, Metadata, Cover price, Wholesale Discounts and Reviews

Scrimpers tip:
All the above can be easily done by you, the author without having to spend any more of your cash. If you'd like to know more about what these mean and how to create them, IngramSpark has a great downloadable resource that walks you through each of the listing requirements and gives you some examples of what works.

Printing

Most self-published authors choose the print-on-demand route as it offers a unique blend of convenience and flexibility while keeping your initial outlay to a minimum. You just upload your manuscript and cover files in pdf format and the printer prints a copy whenever the customer places an order.

Print on Demand also allows you to order an initial stock of books at cost price for your own use. These could be for marketing purposes such as sending to reviewers, potential clients or for sale at the back of the room after a speaking engagement or through your own website. Don't be tempted to buy too many copies; it's better to order between 50-100 and then re-order as you need them.

Scrimpers tip:
Print on Demand is the way to go, and there are several options including Amazon's CreateSpace and Ingram Spark. But pay attention to your shipping costs. If you are ordering more than a few copies, your books are going to be shipped by the carton, so it's always best to order full carton quantities. That way you are not paying to ship empty space. Round up or down to the nearest full carton based on the number of books that you need.

Marketing your book

This is probably the most commonly overlook part of self-publishing. Simply having your book listed on Amazon won't bring a flood of orders to your door. The bad news is that you'll have to do a lot of work to publicise your book, You need to draw it to the attention of potential readers before they will go and buy it!

The good news is that you can do most of this with little or no cash outlay if you have the time. There are a wealth of free marketing opportunities out there including:

- SEO (of both your book website and Amazon listing)
- Organic social media (Facebook, Twitter, LinkedIn, Instagram, Pinterest, etc.)
- Speaking engagements
- Webinars
- Podcasts

The question is how do you generate the invitations and opportunities to promote your book without paying for someone to do it for you?

Scrimpers tip:

Tap into the power of your network and ask them to buy your book, post reviews, and share it with their networks. You can also ask them to put you in touch with book reviewers, bloggers, podcasters, journalists, and radio presenters.

You'll be surprised how helpful people are, but you need to remember to ask (and remind) them to do it!

If you want some more low cost/no cost marketing tips, check out "Book Marketing Made Simple" by Karen Williams

How I Used my Book to Get on the Radio

In an article I wrote back in November (*5 Powerful Ways to Measure Self-Publishing ROI* (https://swatt-books.co.uk/5-powerful-way-to-measure-self-publishing-roi) I mention that a book can be a fantastic way of attracting valuable PR opportunities such as speaking gigs and interviews. Here is a perfect case in point of how easily that can work.

As you probably know I published my first book *Stress-Free Self-Publishing* (https://www.amazon.co.uk/Stress-Free-Self-Publishing-publish-without-losing/dp/1916077609) in May 2020 My launch campaign for the release of that book consisted of doing a 4Sight tour of regional 4Networking meetings in my area where I would visit a networking group as a guest speaker to talk about my book and my experiences of writing and publishing it. This tactic worked extremely well in that I was able to sell nearly 100 copies and triple the number of book contracts I had in my pipeline. But it didn't stop there. I continued to talk about my book whilst networking and still try to 4Sight at least once a month.

In December I gave a 4Sight entitled "How a Book Can Help Your Business" at a 4N meeting in Frome, Somerset. It turned out that one of the ladies at the meeting was Dawn Denton, an active author in the Frome community and host a fortnightly radio show called "World of Writers" on Frome FM. We spoke briefly after the meeting and connected on LinkedIn to stay in touch. Just after the Christmas break, Dawn sent me an email inviting me to be her guest on "World of Writers". That opportunity would probably not have come up had Dawn not seen me speak at the Frome breakfast meeting.

So having written my book (which positioned me as an expert in self-publishing), and taking the time to go out and talk about my book (as part and parcel of marketing both my book and my business), meant that I was offered an amazing opportunity to be a guest on an hour-long radio show that is targeted at my ideal market in a town that has the highest number of writers per capita in the UK! Proof that writing and publishing a book can open various doors and opportunities to you that you may not have had access to before.

The takeaway… talk about your book every chance you get. You never know what opportunities might come your way as a result.

You can listen to the full interview on World of Writers below.
https://www.mixcloud.com/FromeFM/9-world-of-writers-240120-self-publishing-with-sam-pearce-of-swatt-books/

Top 5 Self-Publishing Success Stories, and Lessons You Can Learn from Them

Publishing your book yourself won't guarantee you a bestseller, but these self-publishing success stories prove that success is still possible.

Mention the term self-publishing to some people, and they will tell you that it's vanity publishing and that you'll never achieve a best seller status without the help of an established publishing house. Look at the facts, however, and you will discover that such opinions are simply not correct. Self-publishing won't guarantee you success but, as you will learn when you read the stories behind these five bestselling books, neither is it impossible.

50 shades of Grey - EL James (2011) [29]

Sold 125 million copies in less than 4 years

About "50 Shades of Grey"

50 Shades of Grey is a self-published erotic romance novel by British author EL James. The book was the first instalment of a trilogy and was published in 2011, becoming a record-breaking international bestseller. The book as also made into a film in 2016.

The story behind "50 Shades of Grey."

The Fifty Shades trilogy started life as a serialised story called Master of the Universe, which was inspired by Stephanie Myers vampire novel series Twilight. The author subsequently migrated it to her own website, Fiftyshades.com, after comments relating to its explicit sexual nature.

Sometime afterwards she completely re-wrote it, removed it from her website and then self-published the first of three parts as an eBook. Then in May 2011, released a print-on-demand paperback with the support of an independent Australian publishing house called The Writer's Coffee Shop. The 2nd and 3rd parts were also published by The Writer's Coffee Shop in September 2011 and January 2012 respectively.

Due to the publishers' limited budget, marketing was restricted primarily to reviews by book bloggers and word-of-mouth marketing which, thanks to the demographic of its audience, quickly went 'viral'.

Vintage Books bought the licence to the trilogy and quickly released a new and revised edition in April 2012. At the beginning of August of the same year, Amazon's UK arm announced that 50 Shades of Grey had outsold the complete Harry Potter series in the UK.

Lessons for Authors

Don't be afraid to rework earlier manuscripts. Many famous authors have admitted that the first draft of their novels wasn't up to scratch. If your first attempt isn't well received, consider rewriting it.

Prove the concept first. Many successful authors started by testing out their story ideas via their website and, if the response was positive, went on to invest time and professional help to create a saleable, self-published book.

The Martian by Andy Weir (2011) [3031] [32]

Became a worldwide movie hit grossing over $600M

About "The Martian"
This successful self-published Science fiction book chronicles the story of a NASA astronaut, stranded on Mars and how he survives by using his scientific training.

The story behind "The Martian."
The Martian was written by Andy Weir, a computer programmer and self-confessed space nerd, and was initially published in serial form on Weir's personal website starting in 2009. Weir decided to take the self-publishing route with The Martian because his earlier manuscripts had repeatedly been turned down by literary agents. After numerous requests from readers to make the book available in its entirety, Weir published it in Amazon Kindle format in 2011 with a selling price of just 99 cents. The book quickly became an Amazon bestseller within the science fiction genre, selling in excess 35,000 copies in less than a month. Its online popularity brought it to the attention of numerous mainstream publishers which resulted in deals first for an audiobook version in 2013 followed shortly afterwards by a publishing deal for a hardback version. The hardback version went on to

achieve top twenty status in the New York Times Bestseller list. As if all this wasn't enough, the film rights to the book were bought by Twentieth Century Fox and the film version, starring Matt Damon, released in 2016, went on to gross more than $600 Million worldwide!

Lessons for Authors
Write the best book you can. I have seen blogs which tell you that you can write a bestseller in a few weeks even if you have never written anything before. Really? Writing is a skill, and it takes practice also audiences are discerning and, if your book isn't interesting, relevant and well-written people won't buy it or leave you great reviews. Andy Weir knew about his subject, and he researched it in depth over at least a year. He also made chapters available to his friends and fans via his website. You can bet your bottom dollar that he edited his manuscript based on the feedback he received from his early readers.

The Celestine Prophecy - James Redfield (1993) [33]

Sold 100,000 copies before landing a lucrative publishing deal

About "The Celestine Prophecy"
The Celestine Prophecy is an immensely successful self-help book which explored the nature of humanity's connection to the divine, through a first-person narrative story of spiritual awakening. The book was inspired

by a combination of the psychology of transactional analysis and ancient eastern mysticism.

The story behind "The Celestine Prophecy."

James Redfield grew up in Rural Alabama and studied several Eastern philosophies including Zen Buddhism and Taoism before achieving a master's degree in counselling. He self-published The Celestine Prophecy in 1992 under the imprint Satori Publishing, doing all the promotion, marketing, and distribution himself, and selling more than 100,000 copies in two years. No mean feat given that the internet was still in its infancy back then.

Such was the book's popularity with readers and booksellers alike that Redfield was approached by Warner Books who bought the hardback rights to the Celestine Prophecy for $800,000 and went on to publish the first hardback edition in 1994. The book went on to become the US bestselling book in 1996, selling more than 20 million copies worldwide.

Lessons for Authors

Tap into timing. One way to create a successful book is to write the kind of book that your audience is hungry for. Part of the Celestine Prophecy's success was timing. It was released at a time when there was a global upsurge in people looking for a fresh approach to living a more meaningful, fulfilling, and connected life. Does your book address a clear and present need within your target readership?

Don't neglect the power of connections. James Redfield created a blockbuster book way back in the 90's, without the backing of a big-name publisher or the internet. He was prepared to get out there and talk about his book to anybody willing to listen. He didn't only send out a press release and wait for the orders to roll in and neither should you.

Still Alice by Lisa Genova (2007) [3435]

From rejection to bestseller in less than two years

About "Still Alice"

Still Alice is a novel is about a fictional married woman and mother called Alice who suffers early-onset Alzheimer's disease. This moving story explores how this neurodegenerative disease rapidly progresses, changing Alice's relationship with her family and the world.

The story behind "Still Alice."

Dr Lisa Genova, the author of Still Alice, is an American Neuroscientist with a degree in Biopsychology and a PhD in Neuroscience from Harvard. Lisa's grandmother was diagnosed with Alzheimer's when she was in her 80's. As a result, the author witnessed first-hand as the disease "systematically disassembled the woman I knew as my grandmother."

After researching the topic, Lisa discovered that most of the literature about this illness had been written by the clinicians or the caregiver's point of view rather than the patient's perspective. She wanted to understand what if felt like to have Alzheimer's from the first early symptoms onwards. And, after interviewing and working with many early onset Alzheimer's patients, she wanted to find a way to share that understanding with others, and the Still Alice was the answer.

Genova self-published her first book in 2007 having spent a year unsuccessfully trying to interest literary agents in her manuscript. The last agent she saw warned her that self-publishing would kill her writing career before it had started but thankfully for us all, she ignored their advice and self-published using iUniverse. The way she tells it, "I was selling it out of the trunk of my car and trying to create a buzz."

After a year of incessant guerrilla marketing techniques including Myspace, Goodreads and Shelfari, organising at least two book events every month and attending local book signings, her efforts started to pay off. At this point, she invested in a professional PR agent, and the resulting press and TV buzz led to her finding a sympathetic agent and subsequently lucrative audiobook and paperback deals.

Still Alice subsequently appeared in the New York Times Bestseller List for more than 40 weeks and had been translated into more than 20 languages.

Lessons For Authors

Don't always believe what literary agents tell you. Self-publishing can generate significant sales and can even lead to a mainstream publishing deal if you want it.

Getting published is only the first step. If you really want your book to be a success, you must be prepared to commit to a prolonged period of shameless publicity. This can include a range of diverse activities in including social media, local book signings, speaking events, PR, and award entries.

The Joy of Cooking - by Irma Rombauer (1931) [3637]

18 million copies and eight editions!

About "The Joy of Cooking"
Who would have thought that a book about cooking, written and self-published by an American widow to "uplift the spirits of a nation" during the great depression, would become a worldwide best seller? Irma Rombauer's quirky, culinary classic was the first cookbook to address the challenges facing impoverished housewives, and it continued to adapt to meet the needs of future generations with each new edition.

The story behind "The Joy of Cooking."
Irma Rombauer was not your typical cookbook author. She was an amateur cook and housewife with no recognised culinary qualifications, but she turned this apparent shortcoming into her book's biggest strength. Her lack of expertise naturally allowed her to position herself as a helpful friend in the eye of her readers, rather than as a haughty teacher.

There's not much known as to how and why Irma self-published her cookbook, but one can imagine that trying to secure the support of a mainstream publisher amid a global economic downturn was nigh on impossible. Irma spent a year collating her recipes and then committed half of her life savings, some $3000, to publish 3000 copies of the first edition of "The Joy" as it later affectionately became known.

The design of the book is, in large part, thanks to Irma's daughter Marion, an art teacher, who designed the cover and created the simple line drawings used to illustrate the text. With limited resources, Irma sold the book to her local community, and its reach expanded organically as word of its affordable, no-nonsense recipes and conversational style, spread.

After its initial success, the author produced an updated edition in 1936 and, after multiple rejections, publisher Bobbs-Merrill agreed to publish the book, which went on to become a bestseller with a total of eight editions, the last one being in 1997.

Lessons for Authors
Keep your book current with regularly updated editions. Many authors think that once their book is in print, that their work is done, but this is not always true. As Irma Rombauer knew only too well, times change, and so do the requirements of your readership.

Every author needs a support team. When Irma Rombauer wrote the Joy of Cooking, in 1931, she did so with the enthusiastic support of her son Edgar and her daughter Marion, an art teacher. Make sure you have the right support team in place to help you ensure the success of your book.

Conclusion

And there you have it, Book Boss! A collection of musings from a self-publisher on how to write, publish, and market your own book. We've covered a lot of ground in this book, from the common roadblocks to becoming an author to the benefits of self-publishing as part of an integrated marketing strategy. We've explored the ins and outs of book design, publishing, and authorpreneurship, and I hope you've found the information helpful and inspiring.

If you're reading this book, you're likely someone who is passionate about sharing your ideas, expertise, or story with the world. You may have been thinking about writing a book for a while but didn't know where to start, or you may have already started but are struggling to finish or publish your book. My goal with this book is to give you the tools and inspiration you need to get your book out into the world and make an impact.

Remember, self-publishing is not just about getting your book on Amazon or in bookstores. It's about using your book as a powerful marketing tool to build your brand, establish your credibility, and attract new customers or clients. It's about creating a platform for yourself and your ideas that can lead to new opportunities, partnerships, and speaking engagements. It's about sharing your unique perspective with the world and making a difference.

If you have any questions or want additional support in getting your own book published, please don't hesitate to get in touch with me. As a self-publishing consultant, I'm passionate about helping business owners, thought leaders, and coaches bring their books to life and achieve their goals. Together, we can make your publishing dreams a reality.

How Can I Help?

After reading this book, you might be feeling a bit overwhelmed. You may be thinking to yourself "I just don't have the time or the knowledge to do all of that and still have it do my book justice!"

Well don't panic, I am here to help.

There are several ways in which I can help support you on your publishing journey depending on how involved you need/want me to be:

1. The Book (£14⁹⁹):

My book "Stress-Free Self-Publishing: How to publish your own book without losing the will to live" goes into each of the 12 steps mentioned in this pamphlet in much greater detail. It includes easy to follow illustrated instructions that guide you through the entire process of self-publishing a book.

2. Power Hour Sessions (£60):

Working through the publishing process yourself, but have gotten stuck and need some specific advice? Book a Power Hour session with me to discuss your particular problem and get advice and live support to fix your issue and get your book back on track. To book a session, simply scan the QR code to access my online diary.

3. The Course (£499):

My Stress-Free Self-Publishing Crash Course is for authors who want to learn how to publish their book themselves, but want the reassurance of being taken through the process step by step by a professional. It is delivered as a 6-week drip-fed video course complete with downloadable templates and worksheets to help you through the process of publishing a professional-quality book. During each week of the course, we will focus on a critical step of the self-publishing process. At the end of each week, you will be invited to a live Q&A session with me and your fellow author/

students to ask any questions you may have and to share your insights & gain valuable feedback on your book. The course also includes:

- Free eBook copy of "Stress-Free Self-Publishing"
- Free PDF copy of "Stress-Free Self-Publishing: How to publish your own book without losing the will to live"
- One Year unlimited access to course content
- Lifetime access to private Facebook group (regular live Q&A's, group support, peer review, special offers, guess content, case studies & author interviews)
- Option to book discounted 1:1 Power Hour coaching sessions when stuck

4. Publishing Only (£1,080):

My Publishing Only package is for authors who have print-ready artwork for their book already finished and just want someone to help them get their book over the line and published. The package includes everything from STEP 03 of this pamphlet onwards. Most importantly is that your book will be published completely on your behalf; you will retain 100% of the rights to your book as well as keep 100% of your royalties too.

5. All Inclusive (starting from £2,700):

My All Inclusive package is designed for the author who wants everything done for them in the most professional way possible. It includes every step mentioned in this pamphlet, and will take your book from raw manuscript to being on sale in over 7k book retailers worldwide. And like the Publishing Only package, your book will be published completely on your behalf so you will retain 100% of the rights to your book as well as keep 100% of your royalties too.

Optional marketing packages are also available to bolt onto your main publishing package including 8-week managed PR campaigns and 30-day social media launch campaigns.

What Next?

If you are interested in working with me, or want to discuss how I can help you with your book in more detail, simply scan the QR code below to book a no-obligation digital coffee meeting with me for a time to suit you.

Speaking & Workshops

I am also available for speaking engagements or to run workshops on the power of self-publishing and how it can benefit business owners and thought leaders by raising their profile and accelerating their businesses.

Just Reach Out

If you just fancy a chat about a book idea, the business of being an author or anything book & business related, simply reach out to me:

Web: swatt-books.co.uk
Email: sam@swatt-books.co.uk
Socials:
LinkedIn – www.linkedin.com/in/sampearceswattbooks/
Facebook – www.facebook.com/SWATTBooks
Instagram – www.instagram.com/swattbooks/
YouTube – www.youtube.com/@swattbooks

Endnotes

1. https://www.microsoft.com/typography/ctfonts/WordRecognition.aspx#m1
2. https://en.wikipedia.org/wiki/Word_recognition#Bouma_shape
3. https://en.wikipedia.org/wiki/Word_superiority_effect
4. https://www.microsoft.com/typography/ctfonts/WordRecognition.aspx#m2
5. https://www.microsoft.com/typography/ctfonts/WordRecognition.aspx#m3
6. https://en.wikipedia.org/wiki/Word_recognition#Parallel_recognition_vs._serial_recognition
7. https://en.wikipedia.org/wiki/Word_recognition#Neural_networks
8. https://www.scientificamerican.com/article/when-we-read-we-recognize-words-as-pictures-and-hear-them-spoken-aloud/
9. https://www.microsoft.com/typography/ctfonts/WordRecognition.aspx
10. https://en.wikipedia.org/wiki/Eye_movement_in_reading#Saccades
11. https://dornsife.usc.edu/assets/sites/780/docs/08_ps_song___schwarz_effort.pdf
12. https://www.ncbi.nlm.nih.gov/pmc/articles/PMC3428264/
13. https://baymard.com/blog/line-length-readability
14. https://www.ncbi.nlm.nih.gov/pmc/articles/PMC2772078/
15. https://www.theguardian.com/books/booksblog/2016/mar/21/for-me-traditional-publishing-means-poverty-but-self-publish-no-way
16. https://www.washingtonpost.com/news/arts-and-entertainment/wp/2014/10/01/no-i-dont-want-to-read-your-self-published-book/?utm_term=.ea88b7c37100)
17. http://www.theindependentpublishingmagazine.com/2016/06/the-main-problems-for-self-published-authors-tom-jager-guest-post.html
18. https://www.bayt.com/en/specialties/q/305907/what-is-your-opinion-on-self-publishing-are-these-books-not-as-good-as-books-from-publishing-houses/
19. http://authorkristenlamb.com/2016/04/real-writers-dont-self-publish
20. https://www.theguardian.com/books/booksblog/2016/feb/22/i-didnt-want-to-resort-to-self-publishing-but-its-an-exhilarating-change
21. http://www.miamiherald.com/latest-news/article194448 1.html
22. https://www.goodreads.com/questions/1154334-what-s-your-opinion-on-self-publishing

23. Amazon does offer extended distribution to other retailers, however, there are several restrictions in place, they take a much higher percentage of the cover price, and their distribution network is small since many retailers do not want to deal with a direct competitor.

24. Source: https://copyrightservice.co.uk/copyright/copyright, accessed 18/03/2021

25. Source: https://www.gov.uk/copyright, accessed 18/03/2021

26. Source: https://copyrightservice.co.uk/copyright/p08_berne_convention, accessed 18/03/2021

27. Source: https://www.bl.uk/business-and-ip-centre/articles/fair-use-copyright-explained, accessed 19/03/2021

28. Source: https://www.gov.uk/guidance/exceptions-to-copyright#fair-dealing, accessed 19/03/2021

29. "Fifty Shades of Grey Author Interview E. L. James Before and After ...." 6 Feb. 2015, http://time.com/3697185/fifty-shades-of-grey-e-l-james-interview/. Accessed 30 Jun. 2017.

30. "Adam Savage Interviews 'The Martian' Author Andy Weir - The Talking ...." 11 Jun. 2015, https://www.youtube.com/watch?v=5SemyzKgaUU. Accessed 30 Jun. 2017.

31. "Andy Weir; the man whose space scribblings became The Martian." http://www.telegraph.co.uk/film/the-martian/andy-weir-author-interview/. Accessed 30 Jun. 2017.

32. "The Martian (Weir novel) - Wikipedia." https://en.wikipedia.org/wiki/The_Martian_(Weir_novel). Accessed 30 Jun. 2017.

33. "The Celestine Prophecy - Wikipedia." https://en.wikipedia.org/wiki/The_Celestine_Prophecy. Accessed 30 Jun. 2017.

34. "Still Alice (novel) - Wikipedia." https://en.wikipedia.org/wiki/Still_Alice_(novel). Accessed 30 Jun. 2017.

35. "Interview with Lisa Genova | ALZFORUM." http://www.alzforum.org/early-onset-familial-ad/profiles/interview-lisa-genova. Accessed 30 Jun. 2017.

36. "The Joy of Cooking - Wikipedia." https://en.wikipedia.org/wiki/The_Joy_of_Cooking. Accessed 30 Jun. 2017.

37. "Irma S. Rombauer - Wikipedia." https://en.wikipedia.org/wiki/Irma_S._Rombauer. Accessed 30 Jun. 2017.

www.ingramcontent.com/pod-product-compliance
Lightning Source LLC
Chambersburg PA
CBHW072047110526
44590CB00018B/3065